Stone Wall
and Warm

THE INNS AND OUTS OF EATING IN NEW HAMPSHIRE

Chevion '01

"The Hearth"

Our mission for
Stone Walls and Warm Hearths

The mission of this cookbook is to provide funds to serve the needs of the Town of Hopkinton. This project brings together Hopkinton Woman's Club and community members, using their talents and experiences to create a combination of tantalizing food, evocative words and original art to showcase the lifestyles and traditions of New Hampshire.

The story of "The Hearth" shown on the title page and information regarding the artist can be found on page 246.

To order additional copies of Stone Walls and Warm Hearths:
Write to The Hopkinton Woman's Club
P.O. Box 24
Hopkinton, NH 03229
Toll free telephone or fax:
1-866-HWC-COOK
1-866-492-2665
E-mail: stonewalls@mediaone.net
or visit our web page at
www.stonewalls.org

Cost per copy is $22.95, plus $4.00 shipping and handling.

ISBN 0-9711356-0-6

Library of Congress Catalog Number 2001132580

Printed in the USA by

WIMMER
The Wimmer Companies
Memphis
1-800-548-2537

Briar Hill Stonewalls and Landscape
Cover Art by Byron Carr

This cookbook started to take shape by a process as bi-millennial as the town of Hopkinton, New Hampshire itself: a town select(wo)man led a formal meditation by members of the Hopkinton Woman's Club, ranging in age from young mothers to octogenarians. They agreed to create a cookbook that reflected the look and feel of New Hampshire.

This modern brainstorming session harked back to Hopkinton's eighteenth century beginnings, when women often joined forces across generations to accomplish a common goal. This was, in effect, a present day version of a quilting bee. What follows is the result of two years of their labor: a patchwork of cookery collections stitched together with the flavors of the Granite State that is sure to please your palate. Proceeds from the sale of this book will be used to finance projects in Hopkinton that improve the lives of women, children and the less fortunate.

While all of the artwork in "Stone Walls and Warm Hearths" was created by Hopkinton-area artists and depicts scenes from this central New Hampshire town, the book is a joint effort of cooks, professional chefs, innkeepers, writers and volunteers from across the Granite State. The beautiful town of Hopkinton is representative of hundreds of equally charming villages and towns from Mount Monadnock to the Great North Woods, each with their own picturesque stone walls and warm hearths.

The cover painting is a landscape of Briar Hill Road in Hopkinton. Not far from this pretty rural scene lies Rattlesnake Hill. There, in 1862, Briar Hill Road resident Joseph Barnard oversaw the marathon felling of over a quarter of a million board feet of timber. This was used to build the famous Union man-of-war, the Kearsarge. For two years, the swift, illegally British-built Confederate privateer Alabama had been roaming the seas, wreaking havoc on Northern commerce. The exceptionally tough New Hampshire oak (and her equally tough - mostly New Hampshire - crew) made the Kearsarge more than a match for the Alabama, which she sank off the coast of France in one of the greatest naval actions of the Civil War.

BYRON CARR
Cover Title: "Shadow Walls"

Byron Carr reminisces: "The image for the cover art came to me while prowling Briar Hill Road. I worked quickly — had to — for light changes quickly when painting from nature; it is a focused frenzy to capture the essence of what brings an artist to attempt a painting. One good painting is worth all the failures, black flies and mosquitoes, heat, cold, rain, and wind. The original painting is 10 X 14 inches. The painting from which the cover was taken is 22 X 36 inches."

"I've lived most of my life within 40 miles of the house my grandfather built on the banks of the Contoocook River in Hopkinton, N.H. Good food and art play a large part in my memories. Creamed toast when sick, fresh baked cookies when feeling well, beans, hot dogs and brown bread on Saturday night, and Sunday night after a bath it was homegrown corn popped in the coal furnace. Nothing tastes or smells better than a slow-cooked pot roast dinner on a rainy November afternoon. Such days were filled with drawing and doodling inspired by books, my imagination and memories of expeditions with my father on the river, in the swamp or through the forest and along back roads."

At the age of 42, my life in art had a fresh beginning. I taught myself to draw all over again, got the hang of watercolor, and added oil painting to my repertoire. My work is shown in galleries, and I enjoy teaching and performing demonstrations for groups. By the grace of God, the harder I work the more talented I seem. Time to go. I think I smell pot roast!

Table of Contents

Special Breakfasts   7

Hors d'Oeuvres & Appetizers   39

Soups, Chowders & Stews   53

Salads, Vegetables, Sauces & Condiments   77

Pasta, Grains, Beans & Cheese   99

Poultry & Seafood   115

Meats   133

Pies & Cakes   147

Puddings, Custards & Other Desserts   167

Cookies & Sweets   191

Breads   213

STATE OF NEW HAMPSHIRE

OFFICE OF THE GOVERNOR

JEANNE SHAHEEN
GOVERNOR

July 2001

New Hampshire is a state of towns. The energy that holds us all together is the spirit of community. This spirit fuels many volunteer organizations that power our towns and make our state unique. One such organization is the Hopkinton Woman's Club. For sixty years it has united women and men in community service, friendship and fun.

When the Hopkinton Woman's Club decided to produce a cookbook, they first identified those qualities of their town that made Hopkinton representative of New Hampshire. Two qualities remained constant: a sense of history, and a sense of pride in community. Two features in Hopkinton that symbolize these qualities are Stone Walls, reminding us each day of our rural past, and Warm Hearths, evoking the hearty welcome and genuine hospitality one finds inside our New Hampshire homes.

These qualities are valued throughout New Hampshire. Our reverence for history and our sense of community make our state a wonderful place to live and an attractive destination for visitors. I recommend this cookbook for all those seeking to experience the real "flavor" of New Hampshire. Whether you use the cookbook in your own kitchen, give it as a gift, or take it with you as a souvenir, I am certain that the recipes and stories it contains will be enjoyed for many years to come.

Jeanne Shaheen

Special
Breakfasts

Stonewalls of Jewett House

Stone Walls of Jewett House

This stone wall is one of many that still border country lanes and mark property lines in the town of Hopkinton. Like all the others, it is a kind of memorial to the grit and determination of the people who have wrested a living from our rocky, sandy soil over the last two centuries. To create cropland, the people who wanted to farm here had to clear the land not only of virgin timber (by law leaving the tallest and best for the King), but also of the large stones which "grew" here in great numbers. Each wall thus represents many hours of backbreaking labor.

By the 1830s, however, young people from New Hampshire were starting to leave home to seek richer farmland in the West. This exodus increased after the Civil War, when Hopkinton soldiers had a chance to see how much easier farming could be in other parts of the country. Farmhouses started to go empty, and the forests started to reclaim the hard-won fields. That is why the stone walls meandering through dense woodland today are often the only remaining evidence that these were once cultivated, cleared acres.

Town historian Rose Hanson recalls that the stone wall along their farm on Putney Hill Road served a new purpose in her childhood. When the road between the villages of Hopkinton and Contoocook was being paved, the work crew paid local farmers to bring them stones. Her father thus harvested stones from the double wall (making it into a single wall), hauled them down to Hopkinton village, and sold them to the road crew. The rocks were put into a large machine, ground into gravel, sorted by size, and used in the pavement to make travel easier within the town.

JANE LIST

Jane List has been an Elementary School art teacher for 23 years, with 17 years in Hopkinton. Her preferred media are pen and ink, watercolor and oil. She continues to sell her work on a commission basis, and has done so for over 25 years. In addition to the visual arts, she is passionate about nature, gardening and singing.

Apple-cranberry Granola

Created by Chef Jacqueline Badders of the Inn at Valley Farms
Makes approximately 12 cups

6 cups old-fashioned oats
1 1/4 cups apple juice concentrate
1/2 cup wheat germ
1/2 cup (packed) brown sugar
2 1/2 or 3 tablespoons ground
   cinnamon
1 cup sunflower seeds
1 cup sweetened, flaked coconut
1 1/2 cups sliced almonds
1 tablespoon vanilla extract
1 cup dried cranberries
1/2 cup raisins
1/2 cup golden raisins

Preheat oven to 300 degrees. In a large bowl, combine the first 9 ingredients thoroughly. Divide the mixture between two lightly greased 9 x 13-inch baking pans, and spread evenly. Bake for 20 minutes, then stir gently. Bake for 15 minutes longer, until golden. Watch carefully that the granola on the bottom of the pan doesn't burn. Remove from the oven, let cool slightly, and stir in the cranberries and raisins. Store at room temperature in an airtight container, preferably glass. Or, freeze for up to 1 month.

"Apple juice concentrate replaces oil in this recipe to not only reduce fat content, but add flavor. Great with vanilla yogurt or milk, and perfect to use as a filling for baked apples or baked peaches."

Atwood Inn Breakfast Pudding

Created by Chef Sandi Hoffmeister of the Maria Atwood Inn

Serves 6

butter-flavored vegetable shortening

4 eggs

2 cups milk

1 teaspoon vanilla extract

1 tablespoon maple syrup

1 1/2 cups granola

1 1/2 cups fruit in season
(blueberries, raspberries or
apple slices) tossed with ground
cinnamon

nuts, craisins or raisins, as desired

heavy cream, for serving

Preheat oven to 350 degrees. Grease six 6-ounce baking dishes with shortening. In a large bowl, whisk together the eggs, milk, vanilla, and maple syrup. Divide this among the baking dishes. Add 1/4 cup granola and 1/4 cup fruit to each baking dish and add nuts, craisins or raisins. Stir gently. Bake for 25 to 30 minutes, until set. Serve warm with cream.

Benjamin's Best Sweet Strada
Created by Chef Mimi Atwood of The Benjamin Prescott Inn
Serves 12

24 slices white potato bread, crusts removed

8 eggs

1 quart half-and-half

4 teaspoons vanilla extract

2/3 cup plus 1/2 cup sugar

A couple dashes of freshly grated nutmeg

24 ounces whipped cream cheese

1/2 cup blueberries or raspberries

confectioners' sugar, for dusting

raspberry syrup, for serving

Assemble the night before:

Grease or spray a 15 x 10 x 2-inch glass baking dish. Arrange 12 slices of the trimmed bread in the dish in two rows, overlapping slightly lengthwise to fit the dish.

In a large bowl, whisk together 6 of the eggs, the half-and-half, 2 teaspoons of the vanilla, 2/3 cup of the sugar, and the nutmeg. Pour half of this mixture over the bread. In a medium mixing bowl, beat the remaining 2 eggs with the remaining 2 teaspoons vanilla, 1/2 cup sugar, and cream cheese until well blended. Spread this evenly over the moistened bread. Sprinkle with the berries, and arrange the remaining bread on top. Pour the remaining half of the egg mixture over the bread. Cover tightly with foil, and refrigerate overnight.

Preheat oven to 350 degrees. Bake, covered with foil, for 30 minutes; remove the foil, and continue baking for 20 minutes longer, until puffy and just beginning to brown. It is done when a knife inserted in the center comes out clean. Remove from oven, and let stand for 10 minutes. Dust with confectioners' sugar, and serve hot with raspberry syrup.

Breakfast Casserole

Serves 10 to 12

10 slices bread, cubed

1 pound bacon, cooked until crisp and crumbled

2 cups shredded Cheddar cheese

10 eggs

4 cups milk

4 teaspoons dry mustard

salt and freshly ground pepper to taste

Assemble the night before:

Place the bread over the bottom of a 13 x 9 x 2-inch baking dish or casserole. Sprinkle with the bacon, then the cheese. In a large bowl, whisk together the remaining ingredients thoroughly. Pour the egg mixture evenly into the dish. Cover tightly, and refrigerate overnight.

The next morning, preheat oven to 350 degrees. Bake for 50 to 55 minutes.

Angel Egg Puff

Created by Lynda and Jim Dunwell of the Carter Notch Inn
Serves 8

1/2 cup flour

1/2 teaspoon salt

1 teaspoon baking powder

8 ounces Cheddar cheese, shredded

8 ounces Monterey Jack cheese, shredded

12 eggs

1/2 cup (8 tablespoons) butter, melted and cooled

1 pint (16 ounces) cottage cheese

paprika, if desired

Preheat oven to 350 degrees. In a large bowl, stir together the flour, salt and baking powder, and combine well. Add the shredded cheeses, and toss to combine. In another large mixing bowl, beat the eggs until light. Add the beaten eggs, butter and cottage cheese to the shredded cheese mixture, and stir to combine well. Pour the mixture into a 13 x 9 x 2-inch baking dish, and sprinkle with paprika, if desired. Bake for 30 minutes, until set.

For variety, try adding 1/2 cup of cooked bacon, chopped ham, mushrooms and/or fresh broccoli. This dish holds well over 1 hour.

Eggs Benedict Soufflés

Created by Chef Diane Damato of Ferry Point House Bed & Breakfast
Serves 6

butter
8 eggs
1/2 cup heavy cream
pinch of salt
1 cup finely chopped ham
1 cup shredded Swiss cheese
3 English muffins

For the Hollandaise sauce:
3 egg yolks
2 tablespoons lemon juice
pinch of cayenne pepper
1/4 teaspoon salt
1/2 cup (8 tablespoons) butter

Preheat oven to 350 degrees. Generously butter six 3/4-cup ramekins, and line the bottoms with rounds of wax paper. In a large bowl, whisk the eggs with the cream and salt. Divide the ham and cheese among the ramekins, and then the egg mixture. Set the ramekins in a large, heavy baking pan, and add enough boiling water to come halfway up the side of the ramekins. Bake for about 45 minutes, until the soufflés seem firm in the center when gently shaken. Meanwhile, split, toast, and butter the muffins; keep warm. Prepare the Hollandaise Sauce (below). When the soufflés are done, loosen by running a knife around the sides. Set soufflé on top of toasted English muffin and peel off the wax paper. Spoon Hollandaise Sauce on top, and serve at once.

Prepare the Hollandaise sauce:
Combine the egg yolks, lemon juice, cayenne, and salt in a blender container. Melt the butter, and when it is bubbling, turn the blender on high for 3 seconds. With the motor running, add the butter to the egg mixture in a steady stream. Blend on high for 5 seconds. Serve at once. Makes approximately 1 cup of sauce.

Frittata Puff

Created by Chef Meg Curtis of Stonewall Farm
Serves 8

butter

1 medium zucchini, thinly sliced

10 eggs

1 pint (16 ounces) small-curd cottage cheese

8 ounces Monterey Jack cheese, shredded

8 ounces sharp Cheddar cheese, shredded

1/2 cup flour

1 teaspoon baking powder

1/2 teaspoon salt

1/2 cup (8 tablespoons) butter, melted and cooled

1 tablespoon chopped fresh basil

2 teaspoons chopped fresh oregano

2 tablespoons minced fresh chives

8 cherry tomatoes, halved

Preheat oven to 350 degrees. Butter a 13 x 9-inch baking pan. Cover the bottom of the prepared pan with zucchini. In a large mixing bowl, beat the eggs until lemon-colored. Add the cottage cheese and the shredded cheeses, and beat to combine. Stir in the flour, baking powder, salt, butter and herbs, and combine thoroughly. Pour this mixture over the zucchini. Decorate with the tomatoes, and bake for 35 to 40 minutes, until set. Remove from oven, and let sit for 5 minutes. Serve at once.

"This recipe was given to me 21 years ago by a dear friend. I have altered it so much that it doesn't resemble the original. This can be made with egg substitutes, and lowfat cheeses. And, those of you with herb gardens will love this."

Sara's Egg Dish
Serves 6 to 8

8 ounces sharp Cheddar cheese, shredded

1 tablespoon flour

4 ounces Monterey Jack cheese, shredded

6 to 8 eggs

2/3 cup half-and-half

1 tablespoon Worcestershire sauce

a few drops Tabasco sauce (optional)

10 ounces frozen, chopped spinach, thawed and drained

8 slices tomato

Preheat oven to 350 degrees. In an ungreased, 8-inch square baking dish or quiche dish, toss the Cheddar cheese with the flour. Sprinkle this with the Jack cheese. Beat the eggs with the half-and-half, Worcestershire sauce and Tabasco sauce, and pour this mixture over the cheese. "Float" the spinach over the egg mixture, and top with the tomatoes. Bake for 35 to 40 minutes.

"This was given to me by another innkeeper when my husband and I first opened our bed and breakfast. She said it was easy, and a huge success with her guests. It was with ours, too. This dish can be assembled 24 hours (or the night before) in advance of baking." - *Theresa DeWitt*

Governor's Eggs

Created by Chef Joan DeBrine of Maple Hedge Bed & Breakfast
Serves 8 to 10

10 eggs

1/2 cup flour

1 teaspoon baking soda

1 pint (16 ounces) cottage cheese

1 pound (16 ounces) Monterey Jack
　　cheese, shredded

1 4-ounce can chopped green chilies

1/2 cup (8 tablespoons) butter,
　　melted and cooled

For the sauce:

1 15-ounce can stewed tomatoes

1/2 teaspoon dried basil

Preheat oven to 350 degrees. In a large bowl, beat the eggs to combine well. Beat in the flour, baking soda, cottage cheese, shredded cheese, chilies, and butter. Pour into a greased, 13 x 9-inch pan. Bake for 45 minutes, until the eggs are set. While the eggs cook, make a quick sauce by warming the stewed tomatoes with the basil in a medium saucepan. Serve each portion of eggs with some sauce spooned over.

"This recipe had a different name until we served it to the Governor of New Hampshire (Steve Merrill). He enjoyed it so much we renamed it in his honor."

Christine's Baked Apple Pancake

Created by Chef Christine Crowe of The Crowes' Nest

Serves 4

2 tablespoons unsalted butter

6 tablespoons sugar

1 teaspoon ground cinnamon

3 Granny Smith apples, peeled and sliced

3 eggs

1/2 cup milk

1 tablespoon sour cream or ricotta cheese

1/2 cup flour

1 teaspoon grated lemon zest

confectioners' sugar, for serving

Preheat oven to 400 degrees. In a 10-inch ovenproof skillet, melt the butter over medium-high heat. Stir in the sugar and cinnamon, and then add the apples and sauté just until soft.

In a medium mixing bowl, beat the eggs until frothy. Beat in the milk and sour cream. Add the flour, and beat well. Stir in the lemon zest. Pour the batter over the hot apples in the skillet. Bake for 12 to 15 minutes, until browned and puffy. Dust with confectioners' sugar, and serve at once.

Pumpkin Pancakes

Created by Lynda and Jim Dunwell of the Carter Notch Inn
Serves 3 to 4

1 1/2 cups unbleached flour

2 tablespoons double-acting baking powder

2 tablespoons (packed) light brown sugar

1 teaspoon salt

2 teaspoons ground cinnamon

1 teaspoon ground allspice

1 1/2 cups evaporated milk

1 cup solid-pack canned pumpkin

2 eggs, lightly beaten

1 1/2 teaspoons vanilla extract

1/4 cup bacon drippings

In a large bowl, stir together all the dry ingredients. Add the milk, pumpkin, eggs, vanilla, and bacon drippings, and stir to combine well. Heat a greased griddle over moderate heat until it's hot enough to make drops of water scatter over its surface. Pour the batter on the hot griddle by 1/3-cup measures. Cook for 2 minutes per side, or until the pancakes are golden and cooked through. Serve with maple syrup, honey, or fruit.

The Maria Atwood Inn

A unique experience you will want to enjoy again and again!

Nestled in the heart of the lakes region, this classic 1830 brick federal home with candles in each window invites guests to a time when life was simpler. During the full renovation in 2000, care was taken to preserve original features of the home, such as interior wooden "Indian" shutters, six Count Rumford fireplaces and old, turnkey locks.

This charming bed and breakfast offers seven romantic rooms, each with a private bath, and four with working fireplaces. Antiques are scattered throughout the inn. Quilts on the beds and the aroma of scones baking create a homey atmosphere. Innkeepers Fred and Sandi Hoffmeister offer old-fashioned hospitality, complimentary refreshments in the evening, and a scrumptious full breakfast each morning. The inn is conveniently located for all seasonal sports and activities, including skiing, golfing, hiking, and water activities. Excellent restaurants, historic sites, summer theater and antique shops are all close by. The Maria Atwood Inn is your home away from home.

The Maria Atwood Inn
71 Hill Road
Franklin, NH 03235
603.934.3666
www.atwoodinn.com
Innkeepers Fred and Sandi Hoffmeister

Atwood Inn Oatmeal Pancakes

Created by Chef Sandi Hoffmeister of the Maria Atwood Inn
Makes 10 to 12 pancakes

2 cups rolled oats
1/2 cup flour
1/4 cup sugar
2 teaspoons baking soda
pinch of salt
2 cups buttermilk
2 eggs
1 teaspoon vanilla extract

The night before, combine all ingredients in a large bowl, and stir to combine well. Cover tightly, and refrigerate.

The next morning, remove the batter from the refrigerator. Let it sit at room temperature for 15 to 20 minutes. Additional buttermilk can be added to thin the batter to the preferred consistency. Heat a greased griddle to 350 degrees. (Or, use a nonstick skillet over low heat.) Use 1/3 to 1/2 cup batter for each pancake. The pancakes are ready to flip when the top surface is bubbling nicely, and the pancakes are brown.

Serve with hot maple syrup and ham.

Walnut Pancakes with Glazed Bananas and Spiced Crème Fraîche

Created by Chef de Cuisine Brian Roberge of The Bretton Arms
Serves 6 to 8

For the Spiced Crème Fraîche:

3/4 cup crème fraîche

1/4 teaspoon ground cinnamon

1/8 teaspoon freshly grated nutmeg

1/8 teaspoon ground cloves

1/8 teaspoon ground ginger

salt to taste

For the pancakes:

3/4 cup (12 tablespoons) unsalted butter

1 cup sour cream

1 1/2 cups milk

2 teaspoons vanilla extract

1/3 cup (packed) light brown sugar

1 1/2 cups coarsely mashed, ripe banana

8 eggs

2 cups cake flour

2 cups whole-wheat flour

1 tablespoon plus 1 teaspoon baking powder

2 teaspoons baking soda

1 1/2 teaspoons salt

1 cup chopped walnuts, lightly toasted

1/4 cup (4 tablespoons) clarified, unsalted butter

For the garnish:

6 whole bananas

1/4 cup honey

Prepare the Spiced Crème Fraîche:

In a chilled, medium mixing bowl, beat the crème fraîche on medium speed until it begins to stiffen. Add the remaining ingredients, and continue beating until fairly stiff. Cover tightly and refrigerate.

Prepare the pancakes:

In a heavy medium saucepan, melt the butter over medium-high heat. Add the sour cream, milk, vanilla, and brown sugar, and stir until the sugar dissolves. Remove from heat, and reserve. In a large bowl, combine the mashed bananas and eggs, and stir well. Stir in the butter mixture, and reserve.

In another large bowl, sift together the flours, baking powder, baking soda, and salt. Add about 4/5 of the banana mixture to the flour mixture, and whisk gently to combine. If the resulting batter seems too thick for pancakes, whisk in the remaining banana mixture. Fold in the walnuts.

Walnut Pancakes with Glazed Bananas and Spiced Crème Fraîche continued

Brush a hot griddle with clarified butter, and cook the pancakes until golden brown on each side. While the pancakes cook, peel the remaining bananas, and cut them into diagonal slices. Turn them gently in a medium bowl with the honey to coat well.

To serve, arrange 3 pancakes on each warm serving plate. Top with some of the spiced Crème Fraîche, and sliced bananas, and serve at once.

There Is No Free Lunch in the Live-Free-or-Die State

If you invite a Yankee for dinner, she'll arrive at noon.
If you invite her for supper, that's five o'clock sharp.
If you say, "let's have a lunch," she'll expect a between-meal snack, maybe a cookie and a cup of coffee.
Don't ever invite her for brunch; she'll think you're putting on airs, and will refuse to attend on principle.

Lemon Soufflé Pancakes with Blueberry Maple Syrup

Created by Kim O'Mahoney of the Inn at Portsmouth Harbor
Makes 12 pancakes

1 cup ricotta cheese

3 eggs, separated

1/4 cup (4 tablespoons) unsalted butter, melted and cooled

1 teaspoon vanilla extract

2 teaspoons lemon extract

1/4 cup flour

2 tablespoons sugar

zest of 1 or 2 lemons, if desired

1 cup maple syrup

1 cup blueberries, preferably tiny, wild Maine variety

1 tablespoon blueberry jam

In the large bowl of an electric mixer, beat the ricotta, egg yolks, butter, vanilla, and lemon extract until well blended. Beat in the flour, sugar and lemon zest thoroughly. In another bowl, with clean beaters, beat the egg whites until stiff peaks form. Fold a small amount of the egg whites into the batter to lighten. Fold in the remaining whites gently, taking care not to deflate the mixture. Heat a griddle, and grease it as desired. Using 1/4 cup of the batter for each pancake, cook the pancakes, turning them over when many bubbles appear on the surface.

While the pancakes cook, combine the syrup, berries and jam in a medium saucepan over low heat. When it is hot, serve it over the hot pancakes.

Bill's French Toast

Created by Chef Bill Deppe of The Red Sleigh Inn Bed & Breakfast
Makes 10 to 12 slices

6 eggs, beaten

1 teaspoon vanilla extract

grated zest of 1 orange

1 cup dry pancake mix

2 teaspoons ground cinnamon

1 to 1 1/2 cups milk

1 loaf Italian bread, cut into 1-inch slices

confectioners' sugar and orange slices, for serving

In a large bowl, whisk together the first three ingredients. In a separate bowl, whisk together the pancake mix, cinnamon, and milk until smooth.

Combine the egg mixture and the pancake mixture, and whisk to combine well. Dip the bread slices in the batter and cook on a hot buttered griddle. Be sure to keep the griddle buttered to ensure a crispy crust. Arrange the hot French toast on a platter dusted with confectioners' sugar and garnished with slices of orange. Serve with hot maple syrup, which will enhance the orange flavor.

Blueberry-stuffed French Toast

Created by Chef Meg Curtis of Stonewall Farm
Serves 6 to 8

8 ounces cream cheese, softened

3 tablespoons sour cream

3 tablespoons lemon yogurt

1 large loaf Italian bread, bottom
   crust removed and discarded;
   loaf cut into 1-inch slices

1/2 cup blueberries

10 eggs

1 1/2 cups milk or half-and-half

For the garnish:
confectioners' sugar
additional blueberries

In a small bowl, combine the cream cheese, sour cream and yogurt until smooth. Using a sharp knife, cut a deep pocket into each slice of bread from the trimmed end. Stuff the bread pockets with the berries and the cream cheese mixture. Arrange the stuffed bread slices in a single layer in a baking pan. In a large bowl, beat the eggs and milk until well combined. Pour the egg mixture over the bread, and let sit for 15 minutes. Cook the French toast on a hot, buttered griddle until golden brown. Garnish as desired, and serve at once with hot maple syrup.

"Ten years prior to opening our B & B, a good friend gave us a B & B cookbook. I found a recipe and altered it until I achieved the taste we desired. After we bought Stonewall Farm, we found so many fruits on the property that we tried all of them with this recipe. Raspberry is especially good also. We call this our 'whatever is in season' French toast. This is now a 'signature' breakfast here."

Mom's Cinnamon French Toast with Strawberry-Rhubarb Compote

Created by Chef Barbara Holmes of Mt. Chocorua View House
Serves 6

For the French toast:

3 eggs

1/2 teaspoon ground cinnamon

1/4 teaspoon vanilla extract

pinch of salt

butter

canola or corn oil

1 loaf day-old French bread or cinnamon bread, cut into 1-inch-thick slices

For the Strawberry-Rhubarb Compote:

2 pounds fresh or thawed, frozen rhubarb

2 cups hulled, sliced fresh or frozen (unsweetened) strawberries, thawed

1 teaspoon lemon juice

1/2 to 3/4 cup sugar, to taste

Prepare the French toast:

In a medium bowl, beat the eggs lightly with the cinnamon, vanilla, and salt.

On a griddle or in a large frying pan, melt the butter with the oil over medium-high heat. Dip the bread into the "goop" (as Mom called it), and cook it for several minutes per side, until lightly browned. Serve with Strawberry-Rhubarb Compote, or a good-quality maple syrup.

Prepare the Strawberry-Rhubarb Compote:

If using fresh rhubarb, cut it into 1-inch lengths. In a large saucepan, combine the rhubarb, strawberries and lemon juice over medium-low heat. Let simmer until slightly soft, stirring occasionally. Add the sugar, and continue cooking until thickened to a stew-like consistency.

Baked French Toast

Created by Chef Debbie Howard of the Cabernet Inn
Serves 6

1/4 cup (4 tablespoons) butter

2 tablespoons maple syrup

3 eggs

1/2 cup orange juice

pinch of salt

1/2 teaspoon ground cinnamon

6 slices of day-old French bread (slice about 1-1/2 inches thick)

Preheat oven to 400 degrees. Melt the butter in a 13 x 9 x 2-inch glass baking dish. Stir in the maple syrup. In a medium bowl, beat together the eggs, orange juice, salt and cinnamon. Dip the bread in the egg mixture, and place it in the dish. Pour any remaining egg mixture over the bread. Bake for about 25 minutes until golden brown. Serve at once.

This is an ideal brunch recipe. You can prepare it the night before, and keep in the refrigerator overnight. Just take it out and bake in the morning. Serve with honey, maple syrup, or fruit compote.

Apple Grand Marnier Sauce for French Toast

Created by Breakfast Chef Jennifer Szurley of the Sunset Hill House
Serves 8 to 10

2 cups New Hampshire maple syrup

1/4 cup Grand Marnier liqueur

2 medium apples, peeled if desired, cored, and thinly sliced

In a medium saucepan, bring all ingredients to a slow simmer. Simmer 5 minutes, until the apples are tender.

Just a touch of the sauce will make your French toast the talk of the family breakfast table. Serve warm.

Jackson Cherry Coffee Cake

Created by Lynda and Jim Dunwell of the Carter Notch Inn
Serves 6

For the cake:

1/4 cup dry breadcrumbs

3/4 cup (12 tablespoons) butter, softened

3/4 cup sugar

3 eggs, separated

1 cup flour

1/4 teaspoon salt

1 pound pitted fresh cherries or 2 14 1/2-ounce cans pitted cherries, drained

For the glaze:

3/4 cup confectioners' sugar

1/2 teaspoon almond extract

Prepare the cake:

Preheat oven to 350 degrees. Butter a 10 x 4-inch tube pan and sprinkle with breadcrumbs, and then tap out any excess. In a large mixing bowl, beat the butter and 1/2 cup of the sugar for 2 minutes, until light and fluffy. Add the egg yolks, and beat for about 2 minutes longer until fluffy. Beat in the flour and salt. In a medium mixing bowl, with clean beaters, beat egg whites until foamy. Beat in the remaining 1/4 cup sugar, 2 tablespoons at a time, and beat until stiff. Gently fold the beaten egg whites into the batter. Spread the batter into the pan, place the cherries on top, and push some into the batter. Bake for 35 to 40 minutes, until a toothpick inserted near the center comes out clean. Remove from oven, and let cool for 5 minutes before removing from pan. Top with glaze.

For the glaze:

Mix the confectioners' sugar, almond extract, and 2 to 3 teaspoons water until glossy.

Jewish Coffee Cake

Created by Chef Debbie Howard of the Cabernet Inn
Serves 12 to 14

1/2 cup (8 tablespoons) butter, softened

1 cup granulated sugar

2 eggs

2 cups sifted cake flour

1 teaspoon baking powder

1 teaspoon baking soda

1 cup sour cream

1 teaspoon vanilla extract

1/2 cup (packed) brown sugar

1 teaspoon ground cinnamon

1/2 cup chopped walnuts

Preheat oven to 350 degrees. In a large mixing bowl, cream the butter, sugar and eggs. In a separate bowl, sift together the cake flour, baking powder and baking soda. Add this mixture to the egg mixture, and beat until smooth. Fold in the sour cream and vanilla. Pour half the batter into a well-greased 8-cup tube pan. In a small bowl, combine the brown sugar, cinnamon and nuts. Sprinkle half the nut mixture over the batter. Add the rest of the cake batter, and top with the remaining nut mixture. Bake for 45 minutes, until a toothpick inserted near the center comes out clean. Remove from oven, and let cool completely before unmolding.

"This recipe was one of my mother's favorites. She would often serve it at afternoon summer tea parties that she hosted in our yard for the neighborhood ladies and their children."

Streusel-topped Blueberry Cake
Created by Chef Debbie Howard of the Cabernet Inn
Serves 12

For the cake:

3 tablespoons vegetable shortening

1 cup sugar

1 egg

1 3/4 cups sifted flour

2 teaspoons baking powder

1/2 teaspoon salt

1 cup milk

1 1/2 cups blueberries, washed and drained

For the streusel:

1/2 cup flour

1/2 cup sugar

2 tablespoons margarine, softened

1 teaspoon ground cinnamon

Preheat oven to 350 degrees. Grease and flour an 11 x 7 x 2-inch or 9 x 9 x 2-inch baking pan. In a medium mixing bowl, cream the shortening and sugar; beat in the egg. Sift together the flour, baking powder, and salt. Add the dry ingredients to the egg mixture alternately with the milk, beating well after each addition. Toss the blueberries gently with a little flour (to keep them from sinking) and stir them into the batter. Pour the batter into the prepared pan. In a small bowl, combine the streusel ingredients until crumbly. Sprinkle the batter evenly with the streusel. Bake for about 40 minutes, until a toothpick inserted near the center comes out clean.

"This recipe is a family favorite, and is especially good with fresh blueberries. It smells divine while baking, and once served, there are rarely leftovers. Frozen or canned, drained berries can be used."

Rhubarb Coffee Cake

Created by Chef Bonnie Webb of The Inn on Golden Pond
Serves 10 to 12

2 cups flour

1 1/4 cups sugar

1 teaspoon baking soda

1 teaspoon salt

1/4 teaspoon ground cloves

1 teaspoon ground cinnamon

1/4 teaspoon ground allspice or
  grated nutmeg

2 eggs

1/4 cup vegetable oil

1/3 cup milk

2 generous cups diced rhubarb

For the topping:

1/4 cup (4 tablespoons) butter,
  softened

1/2 cup (packed) light brown sugar

2/3 cup flour

3/4 cup sweetened, flaked coconut

1/4 cup chopped walnuts

Preheat oven to 350 degrees. Grease a 13 x 9 x 2-inch baking pan. In a medium bowl, sift together the dry ingredients. In another bowl, whisk the eggs and oil together well. Stir this into the dry ingredients. Add the milk and combine well. Fold in the rhubarb. Spread the batter evenly in the prepared pan.

Prepare the topping:

In a medium bowl, cream the butter and sugar together. Add the flour, coconut and nuts. Mix well. Spread the topping over the batter, and bake for 50 minutes, until a toothpick inserted near the center comes out clean.

"Fresh rhubarb from the inn's back yard is used in this recipe. Even people who think they don't like rhubarb love this coffee cake."

Overnight Coffee Cake

Serves 12

For the batter:

2 cups flour

1 teaspoon baking soda

1 teaspoon baking powder

1/2 teaspoon salt

3/4 cup granulated sugar

1/2 cup (packed) brown sugar

1 teaspoon ground cinnamon

2/3 cup (11 1/2 tablespoons) butter or margarine, melted and cooled

1 cup buttermilk

2 eggs

For the topping:

1/2 cup (packed) brown sugar

1/2 cup chopped pecans

1 teaspoon ground cinnamon

Grease and flour a 13 x 9 x 2 -inch baking pan. In a large mixing bowl, combine the batter ingredients. Beat at low speed until moistened, then at medium speed for 3 minutes. Spoon into prepared pan, cover tightly, and refrigerate for 8 to 12 hours.

Preheat oven to 350 degrees. In a small bowl, combine the topping ingredients, and sprinkle evenly over the batter. Bake for 30 to 35 minutes, until a toothpick inserted near the center comes out clean.

Adapted from *Culinary Treasures*, a cookbook by The Avid Gardners, Hilton Head Plantation, Hilton Head Island.

Yankee Grit(s)

Created by Chef Mimi Atwood of The Benjamin Prescott Inn
Serves 6 to 8

1 cup quick-cooking grits

1/2 teaspoon salt

1/2 cup (8 tablespoons) butter

1 cup grated sharp Cheddar cheese

6 eggs

1/2 pound bacon, cooked until crisp,
   then crumbled

1/2 cup half-and-half

2 tablespoons chopped, fresh parsley
   (or 1 teaspoon dried)

Preheat oven to 350 degrees. Cook the grits according to the package directions. Over gentle heat, add the salt, butter and cheese, and stir until they have melted. Remove from heat, and let cool a little. In a medium bowl, beat 2 of the eggs until foamy; stir thoroughly into the grits. Pour the mixture into a 2-quart casserole. Set aside about 1/2 cup of the bacon; sprinkle the remaining bacon over the mixture.

In a medium mixing bowl, beat the remaining 4 eggs with the half-and-half and parsley, and pour this over the bacon and grits. Bake until golden for 30 to 45 minutes. Top with the reserved bacon, and serve hot.

Cheese-baked Apples

Created by Chef Diane Damato of Ferry Point House Bed & Breakfast

Serves 6 to 8

6 to 8 large Cortland apples
8 ounces cream cheese, softened
1 egg
1/2 cup sugar
1 teaspoon vanilla extract
ground cinnamon

Preheat oven to 350 degrees. Peel away 1 inch of the skin from around the top of each apple. Core the apples, and remove some of the pulp, leaving a shell about 3/4 inch thick. In a small bowl, combine the cream cheese, egg, sugar, and vanilla. Beat until smooth and creamy. Divide the filling among the apples, and place each apple in a ramekin. Place all ramekins in a large baking pan, and pour in enough boiling water to reach approximately 1/2 inch up the side of the pan. Sprinkle the apples with cinnamon. Bake for 45 minutes, until the apples are uniformly soft. When the apple skins split, and the filling has slightly browned on top, they are done. Serve, and enjoy the compliments!

"Living in an area with many apple orchards, I enjoy preparing this fruit course in the fall, when apples are freshly picked. I use only Cortland apples, as they 'stand up' and hold together best. You will get rave reviews when serving these!"

Poached Pears with Raspberry Sauce

Created by Chef Diane Damato of Ferry Point House Bed & Breakfast

Serves 6

cold water

2 tablespoons lemon juice

6 firm, ripe Anjou or Bartlett pears, peeled (with stems left on)

For the Raspberry Sauce:

3 cups fresh raspberries, unsweetened, or 1 bag frozen, unsweetened raspberries, thawed

1 cup sugar

1 teaspoon lemon juice

6 fresh mint sprigs, for serving

Fill a large pan with cold water, and add the lemon juice. Place the pears in the acidulated water as soon as they are peeled, being sure the pears are well covered. Cover the pan, and heat on high until water starts to boil. Let boil for a moment, then uncover, reduce heat, and let simmer until the pears are tender. Remove the pears from the pan, and place them standing up in a dish. Cover tightly with plastic wrap, and refrigerate overnight. Prepare the Raspberry Sauce (below), cover tightly and refrigerate. To serve, set each pear upright in dish, drizzle with Raspberry Sauce, and garnish with mint.

Prepare the Raspberry Sauce:

Purée the raspberries in a food processor or blender. Press the purée through a fine sieve to remove the seeds. Put the sieved purée in a small saucepan, and stir in about half of the sugar. Cook over moderate heat, stirring until the sugar dissolves and the sauce is hot. Stir in the lemon juice, and add enough of the remaining sugar to sweeten the sauce to taste. Let cool, and refrigerate. (Makes 1 to 1 1/2 cups.)

Barb's Baked Bananas

Created by Chef Barbara Holmes of Mt. Chocorua View House

Serves 6

1/4 cup (4 tablespoons) butter

2 to 3 tablespoons lemon juice

6 ripe, firm bananas, peeled and quartered

1/4 cup (packed) brown sugar

3/4 teaspoon ground cinnamon

For the garnish:

orange or lemon zest

sweetened, flaked coconut

fresh mint sprigs

Preheat oven to 375 degrees. Put the butter in a shallow baking dish just large enough to hold the bananas in one layer. Place in the oven until the butter is melted. Remove from oven, and stir in the lemon juice. Place the quartered bananas in the dish, and gently turn to coat with butter. Sprinkle with brown sugar and cinnamon. Bake for 12 to 15 minutes, turning once, until bubbly. Remove from oven, and transfer to small serving dishes. Garnish, and serve warm.

"This is a great start to a fall or winter breakfast and a wonderful dessert when topped with a scoop of frozen yogurt or ice cream!"

How to Pronounce New Hampshire Town Names Like a Native

Berlin: Not Ber-LIN like the city in Germany, but BER—lin and in Brrrr, it's some cold up here come January.

Concord: Not Con-cord like the fast plane or a peace agreement, but Conk-id or, some say, Con-curd, as in "Napoleon conquered many countries."

Contoocook: One reply to "You can't cook!" is "Con-too-cook."

Coos Junction: Not Coos like what doves do, but Co as in co-worker and os as in osprey. And everybody knows how to pronounce junction. It's junk + shin.

Danbury: Place a curse on some cheese as in damn-brie.

Gilmanton: Peyton Place

Sandwich, East Sandwich, North Sandwich, and South Sandwich: There is no West Sandwich, but if there were, the "d" would be silent as in the others.

Weare: Where?
No. Weare: Nowhere.

Hors d'Oeuvres & Appetizers

Town Hall

Town Hall

The picturesque Town Hall, featured quadrennially on national television during the hullaba-loo otherwise known as the New Hampshire primary, is rather new by Hopkinton stan-dards. It dates back only to 1874, when it was built to replace the courthouse, which burned the year before.

The original courthouse was constructed on this site in 1796 during the glory years of Hopkinton, when it was a both a half-shire town (one of two "seats" of what was then Hillsboro County), and one of the communities that took turns being the state capital. This meant that not only was county business transacted in the building, but also the peripatetic state legislature, the Superior Court and the Court of Common Pleas met there on a regular basis. Two governors were inaugurated there — twice each. Because of these important government activities, Hopkinton's population grew dramatically, and lawyers and other professionals built beautiful homes in Hopkinton Village.

Unfortunately, this prosperity was dampened when, in 1819, Concord became the perma-nent capital. Soon thereafter, Hopkinton also lost its half-shire status by the creation of Merrimack County. Even so, the former senate chamber and courtroom did not go empty: for almost half a century (1827-1873) Hopkinton Academy — with male and female students — operated there.

After the new Town Hall was built, Town Meeting was held there every March until the voting population could no longer squeeze inside. Surprisingly, even after women gained the right to vote, the crowd did not immediately double in size. Town historian Rose Hanson recalls that it took quite a while for female voters to get up the gumption to attend Town Meeting. Instead, the women cooked a big meal upstairs at the Town Hall while the men wrangled downstairs. They did, however, make those weary male voters pay for their food.

SALLY CHASE

Sally Chase graduated from the Rhode Island School of Design. (When asked by teachers there where she had previously studied drawing, she explained it was years of practice during math, French and history classes.) Her work is exhibited by a gallery in South Brooksville, Maine, and has been shown at the New Hampshire Antiquarian Society, and the Concord Public Library. She has always loved drawing, and is never without pencil and paper, whether on a bird walk in New Hampshire or walking in England.

Gougères (Cheese Puffs)

Makes 36 gougeres

1 cup water

5 tablespoons butter

1 teaspoon salt

1/4 teaspoon freshly ground pepper

1/4 teaspoon freshly grated nutmeg (commercially grated can be substituted, but it won't be as good)

1 cup flour

1 cup shredded best-quality (preferably imported) Swiss cheese, or Gruyère cheese

5 eggs, at room temperature

Preheat oven to 425 degrees. In a medium saucepan, combine water, butter, salt, pepper and nutmeg over medium-high heat. Bring to a boil. When the butter has melted, remove from heat. Add the flour all at once, and beat with a wooden spoon until the mixture pulls from the sides of the pan. Add the cheese, and mix thoroughly. Beat in 4 of the eggs one by one, incorporating each thoroughly before adding the next. Beat until mixture is shiny and smooth.

Grease cookie sheets, and drop the mixture by small spoonfulls onto the sheets. Mix the remaining egg with 1/2 tablespoon water, and brush this lightly over the tops of gougères before baking. Bake in the upper third of the oven for about 20 minutes, until golden brown. Serve at once.

Bake these puffs close to serving time. They are best served right away, but can be reheated at 375 to 400 degrees for about 3 minutes.

Hot Swiss Wedges

Created by Chef Joan DeBrine of Maple Hedge Bed & Breakfast
Makes 16 wedges

1 cup shredded Swiss cheese
1 tablespoon grated onion
enough mayonnaise to moisten
2 English muffins, split
paprika

In a medium bowl, stir together the cheese, onion, and enough mayonnaise to make a moist mixture. Divide the mixture among the English muffin halves, and spread evenly. Sprinkle with paprika. Broil until bubbly and golden brown. Let cool slightly, and cut each half into 4 wedges. Serve warm.

"Each evening at Maple Hedge we serve wine with our local smoked Swiss cheese (Fanny Mason Farmstead Swiss Cheese). At the end of the week there are many small pieces of cheese left over. I developed this appetizer to use these pieces of cheese. The guests love it."

Hot Crab Wedges

Created by Chef Lea Greenwood of the Eastman Inn
Serves 12

6 ounces Cheddar cheese, shredded
1 tablespoon butter
1 1/2 cups crabmeat, picked over for cartilage
1 8-ounce container soft cream cheese with onions and chives
1/2 teaspoon dried dill weed
6 pimento-stuffed olives, sliced
1 3-ounce jar chopped mushrooms, drained
1/2 cup mayonnaise
6 English muffins, split

Preheat oven to 350 degrees, or turn on the broiler. Combine all ingredients except muffins; spread mixture on muffins. Bake (or broil) for 12 to 15 minutes, until bubbly. Let cool slightly, and then cut each muffin into 6 wedges. Serve warm.

Willow Bend Boursin

Makes about 3 cups

1 cup (16 tablespoons) butter, softened

1 pound cream cheese, softened

3 or 4 cloves garlic, minced

1/2 teaspoon dried basil

1/2 teaspoon dried oregano

1/2 teaspoon dried marjoram

In a small or medium mixing bowl, or in a food processor fitted with the steel blades, combine all the ingredients thoroughly.

This is a wonderful soft cheese for dipping, spreading or flavoring other recipes. It freezes well. Low-fat margarine and cream cheese can be substituted, but do not freeze if either or both are used.

Lobster Bomb

Created by Chef Michael Hamm, Sr. of Whitney's Inn
Serves 8

2 pounds cooked lobster meat, picked over for cartilage, and coarsely chopped

2 tablespoons mayonnaise

splash of fresh lemon juice

pinch of dried dill weed

freshly ground pepper to taste

8 10-inch flour tortillas

1/4 cup (4 tablespoons) butter, softened

granulated garlic

freshly grated Parmesan cheese

In a medium bowl, combine the lobster, mayonnaise, lemon juice, dill, and pepper, and stir gently until well mixed. Set aside. Heat a large skillet until hot. Arrange tortillas in the skillet in a single layer (you will have to prepare the tortillas in batches). Brush each tortilla with butter, and then sprinkle each with a pinch of granulated garlic and Parmesan. Flip the tortillas over, and cook until the cheese begins to brown. As each tortilla is browned and ready, remove it from the skillet and quickly spread 1/8 of the lobster mixture over the unbuttered side. Roll the filled tortillas as for a burrito, folding in the sides. Serve at once.

"Developed for a particulary fussy customer who was 'sick of the @#!! no-taste lobster rolls' then listed as an appetizer on our menu."

Shrimp Spread

Serves 10 to 12

1 10 3/4-ounce can condensed cream of tomato soup

8 ounces cream cheese

1 envelope gelatin, softened in 1/2 cup water

1 cup finely chopped onion

1 cup mayonnaise

9 ounces canned shrimp, drained

In a medium saucepan, combine the soup concentrate and cream cheese over low heat. Stir until thoroughly combined. Remove from heat, and stir in the remaining ingredients. Transfer the mixture to a 4-cup mold. Cover tightly, and refrigerate for at least 8 hours.

"I always made this for a snack for people who came to Contoocook's Artisans' Craft Fair. Serve with crackers." -*Nan Winzeler*

Tomato-stuffed Mushrooms

Serves 2

6 large, button mushrooms (about 6 ounces), stems trimmed and reserved

1 tablespoon unsalted butter

2 scallions, finely chopped

1 tablespoon sun-dried tomatoes (packed in oil), drained and minced

1 tablespoon fine, dry breadcrumbs

2 tablespoons freshly grated Parmesan cheese

salt and freshly ground pepper to taste

Preheat oven to 375 degrees. Lightly grease a small baking dish. Finely chop the reserved mushroom stems. In a heavy skillet, melt the butter over medium-low heat. When it is hot, add the chopped stems and scallions, and cook, stirring until the stems are very tender. Stir in the tomatoes, breadcrumbs, 1 tablespoon of the cheese, and salt and pepper. Divide the mixture among the mushroom caps, mounding it slightly, and sprinkle with the remaining 1 tablespoon cheese. Arrange the filled mushrooms in the prepared dish. Bake for 10 to 12 minutes, until piping hot.

Fabulous Mushroom Dip

Serves 10 to 12

1 tablespoon butter or margarine

1 small or medium onion, chopped

3 12-ounce packages fresh button mushrooms, cleaned, trimmed, and sliced

1/2 cup mayonnaise

2 cups shredded sharp Cheddar cheese

1/4 pound bacon, cooked until crisp, and crumbled

Preheat oven to 350 degrees. In a large skillet, melt the butter over medium-high heat. Add the onion, and sauté briefly. Add the mushrooms, reduce the heat, and cook slowly until they are soft. Drain off any liquid, and cook a few minutes longer. Remove from heat.

Stir mayonnaise into the mushroom mixture, and scrape the mixture into a 9-inch shallow baking dish, such as a quiche dish. Cover with cheese, and sprinkle with bacon. Bake for 30 to 40 minutes, until bubbly. Serve at once with crackers.

Speaking of Smart

Speaking of smart, the neighbor was complaining the other day about his Cousin Carl and how Carl borrowed his maroon pick-up truck two years ago and the neighbor said: "Carl, it leaks oil bad, so be sure and keep it oiled up or the engine will seize and that'll be the end of it." Well, Carl didn't check the oil as often as he should have when he was moving his stuff out of the big house into the little apartment in Pittsfield where his soon-to-be-ex-wife thought he ought to resettle. And the engine seized. The truck died. Carl was sorry. The neighbor was upset. It had been a old truck and some rusty, but it had worked good for tooling around town, hauling wood, dump runs and so forth.

"Carl invited me up to the old Barker place to go bird hunting on Saturday," the neighbor told Perley.

"And you agreed to it?" Perley said, surprised.

The neighbor shook his head. "I don't know why," he said. "He's already shot me twice."

Chesterfield Inn

A Luxurious Country Inn

Resting on a hillside with sweeping views of the Connecticut River Valley and the Green Mountains of Vermont, the Chesterfield Inn is a luxurious country hotel set amid lush gardens. Your comfort and privacy are the first consideration of owners Phil and Judy Hueber. Each of the fifteen guest rooms is richly appointed and generously proportioned, with an inviting sitting area. Many of the guest rooms include a wood-burning or gas fireplace, opulent bath with whirlpool, and a private deck or terrace where you can drink in the stunning views and the scent of flowers from the Inn's perennial gardens. The gardens yield a rich harvest of herbs which, combined with produce from local farms and other regional ingredients, are featured in the Inn's contemporary cuisine. Each evening, the setting sun, panoramic views, fresh-cut flowers and candlelight provide the perfect backdrop for an incredible dining experience. The dining rooms, parlor and terrace are also the ideal setting for small parties and celebrations. As tempting as it is to linger at this private oasis for your entire stay, the Inn is just a short and scenic drive to Brattleboro, Vermont and Keene, New Hampshire, as well as the many areas of cultural, historical and recreational interest in southwestern New Hampshire, southern Vermont and northern Massachusetts.

Chesterfield Inn
PO Box 155
Chesterfield, NH 03443
603.256.3211
800.365.5515
www.chesterfieldinn.com
Owners Phil and Judy Hueber

Acorn Squash Crepes

Created by Chef Glenn Gonyea of the Chesterfield Inn
Serves 6 (2 crepes per serving)

For the filling:

2 small acorn squash, halved lengthwise and seeded

1 tablespoon olive oil

1 3/4 to 2 cups ricotta cheese

1/4 cup (packed) brown sugar

1 teaspoon ground cinnamon

1 teaspoon freshly grated nutmeg

salt and freshly ground pepper to taste

1/2 cup (8 tablespoons) butter, softened

1/4 cup maple syrup

For the crepes:

3 eggs

1 1/2 cups milk

1 cup flour

1 tablespoon butter, melted

1 teaspoon salt

For the garnish:

1/2 cup chopped walnuts

Prepare the filling:

Preheat oven to 400 degrees. Line a baking sheet with aluminum foil. Rub the acorn flesh with the oil, and put the squash, cut side down, on the prepared baking sheet. Bake for 50 minutes, until tender. (While squash bakes, prepare crepe batter, below). Remove squash from oven, and scrape the flesh into a medium bowl. Mash with the ricotta, sugar, cinnamon, nutmeg, salt, and pepper until smooth. Set aside. In a small mixing bowl, cream the butter until light. Drizzle in the maple syrup, and beat until fluffy. Set aside.

Prepare the crepes:

Put all the crepe ingredients in a blender, and blend on high speed for 30 seconds. Scrape down the sides of the blender container with a rubber spatula, and blend again until smooth. Refrigerate the batter for 1 hour.

With a crepe pan sprayed with nonstick cooking spray, cook the crepes, using 1/4 cup batter for each. Preheat oven to 400 degrees. To assemble, roll each crepe with about 1/3 cup of the squash mixture. Fit the filled crepes snugly into a baking dish. Dot with the maple butter, and sprinkle with the nuts. Bake for 10 to 15 minutes, until hot. Serve at once.

Mountain Lake Inn's Meatballs

Created by Tracy Foor of the Mountain Lake Inn
Makes 30 meatballs

For the meatballs:
2 pounds ground beef
1 egg, beaten
1 1-ounce envelope onion soup mix
2 tablespoons Worcestershire sauce
3 tablespoons water
30 stuffed green olives or pitted ripe olives

For the sauce:
1 12-ounce bottle chili sauce
1 18-ounce jar grape jelly
1/4 cup lemon juice
3 tablespoons prepared horseradish

Preheat oven to 375 degrees.

Prepare the meatballs:

In a large bowl, thoroughly combine the beef, egg, soup mix, Worcestershire sauce, and water. Mold some of the mixture around each olive to shape a meatball. Place the meatballs in a single layer in a shallow baking dish, and bake for 20 minutes.

Prepare the sauce:

In a medium bowl, combine the sauce ingredients. Pour the sauce over the meatballs, and bake for 10 minutes longer, or until the sauce thickens a little. Transfer the meatballs and sauce to a chafing dish or slow cooker for serving.

"I made this appetizer for a wedding rehearsal dinner; the guests liked it so much they wanted this as their main entrée! "

Taco Dip

Serves 8 to 10

8 ounces cream cheese, softened

8 ounces prepared salsa

1 medium onion, finely chopped

1 medium green bell pepper,
　finely chopped

1 medium tomato, cored
　and chopped

5 ounces Cheddar cheese, shredded

1 4-ounce can sliced black olives

Spread the cream cheese over the bottom of an 8- or 9-inch pie plate. Top with half of the salsa, then the onion, and the bell pepper. Cover with the remaining salsa, then layers of tomato, cheese, and finally olives. Cover tightly and refrigerate.

Bring to room temperature before serving. Serve with corn chips.

Skinny Chicken

Created by Chef Michael Hamm, Sr. of Whitney's Inn
Serves 8

8 good-sized baked potatoes, the flesh scooped out and reserved for another use

1/4 cup (4 tablespoons) butter or margarine

1/2 teaspoon minced garlic

1 medium onion, diced

1/2 pound medium button mushrooms

1 pound broccoli florettes, trimmed to a uniform size

2 pounds skinless, boneless chicken breasts, cut into bite-size pieces

2 ounces freshly grated Parmesan cheese

1/4 cup dry white wine

1/2 cup prepared Caesar dressing

For the garnish:

4 strips bacon, cooked until crisp

8 ounces Cheddar cheese, shredded

Preheat oven to 300 degrees. Set the potato shells, cut side up, on a baking sheet, and put them in the oven to warm; do not let them brown much. Meanwhile, in a large skillet, melt the butter over medium-high heat. When it is hot, add the garlic, onion, mushrooms, and broccoli, and sauté briefly. Add the chicken, and continue to sauté until the chicken just begins to brown. Add the Parmesan, and toss. Deglaze the pan with the wine. Stir in the Caesar dressing, reduce the heat to medium, and continue cooking for 5 minutes, stirring frequently.

Remove the potatoes from the oven, and arrange on serving plates. Fill them with the chicken mixture. Crumble bacon over the top of each, sprinkle with cheese, and serve at once.

Excellent as either a large appetizer or a casual entrée.

Soups, Chowders & Stews

Kimball Farm

Kimball Farm

Some of the earliest English settlers in Hopkinton were Aaron and Susanna Kimball, who came here from Massachusetts in 1740. Their son, Abraham, was the first English child actually born in the town — then called Number Five.

At first, the family lived near what is now Hopkinton Village in a garrison house, one of the three homes in town which were meant to be fortified shelters where neighbors gathered in case of Indian attack. During the long conflict known as the French and Indian Wars (1744-1763), France sought to undermine the morale of English settlers by encouraging such attacks. They later rewarded their Indian allies for kidnapping settlers living on the frontier and for bringing them to Canada, where they would be held for ransom. A number of Hopkinton settlers were so captured, and some died in captivity.

Young Abraham Kimball nearly shared such a fate. One morning in 1753, while driving his father's cow from Putney Hill towards Kimball's Garrison, he was captured by Indians. Soon the band encountered another unlucky boy, Samuel Putney, and took him prisoner, too. Luckily, the boys' story had a happy ending. Soon after heading north, their captors made the mistake of trying to bushwhack the Flanders families, whose men were veterans of the famous Rogers' Rangers expeditions against the Indians. When a wary Flanders dog gave the alarm, the Englishmen managed to surprise the Indians, and gained the boys their freedom.

In 1771, the King of England granted Aaron Kimball the land for this farm on Beech Hill. Kimball descendants live there still. Although several generations were dairy farmers, current Kimballs now sell flowers, ice cream, home-baked bread, maple candy, and other treats in what used to be the cow barn. Another barn is sometimes used for a seriously scary Hallowe'en haunted house.

ELLEN DAVIS

The creative side of Ellen Davis' persona has been in overdrive for as long as she can remember. As a child, she enjoyed artistic projects in watercolors, tempera, and oils, as well as fabric, art and sewing. After college and a teaching career, she explored other media, and continued her study of fine art with classes at the New Hampshire Institute of Art. Her current interests can be found in folk art and faux art, painting murals in client's homes.

Sweet Chestnut Soup

Created by Chef de Cuisine Brian Roberge of the Bretton Arms
Serves 4

4 cups roasted, peeled chestnuts

4 cups homemade chicken broth, or 2 cups canned broth and 2 cups water

2 bay leaves

coarse or Kosher salt

1 cup milk

3 tablespoons heavy cream

In a medium saucepan, combine the chestnuts, broth, bay leaves, and salt to taste over medium-high heat. Bring to a boil, skimming the surface as needed, and let boil for 10 to 15 minutes, until the chestnuts are very tender. Remove from heat, and let cool slightly.

Remove and discard the bay leaves. Transfer the chestnuts and broth to a blender container (or the workbowl of a food processor fitted with the steel blade). Measure the broth; if there are not at least 2 cups, add enough additional broth to make up 2 cups total. Process the broth and chestnuts until the mixture is as smooth as butter. Return the mixture to the saucepan, and stir in the milk and cream until the soup has the desired consistency — you may want to add more broth or milk for a light, smooth soup. (Chestnut Soup always seems to thicken between the stove and the table, so add slightly more liquid than you think you need.) Warm the soup gently until it is piping hot, and season at the table with salt. Serve hot or warm.

Lynda's Wonton Soup

Serves 4

1 egg yolk

2 tablespoons dried breadcrumbs

1/4 cup plus 1 tablespoon chopped onion

1/4 pound lean ground pork

24 wonton skins

1 tablespoon butter

1 carrot finely chopped

4 cups chicken broth

2 tablespoons soy sauce

1 small zucchini, shredded

In a small bowl, lightly beat the egg yolk. Add the breadcrumbs, 1 tablespoon of the onion, and the pork, and mix thoroughly.

Place 1 teaspoon of this pork filling in the center of each wonton skin, and fold the corners in, as for a diaper. Slightly wet the corners so the dough wrapping will make a tight seal. Reserve the filled wontons.

In a medium saucepan, melt the butter over medium-high heat. Add the remaining 1/4 cup onion and the carrot, and sauté until the onion is soft. Add the broth and soy sauce, and bring to a boil. Add the zucchini and wontons, and reduce the heat. Let simmer for 15 minutes, until the pork is thoroughly cooked.

Carrot and Leek Soup

Courtesy of Spring Ledge Farm
Serves 4 to 6

3 tablespoons olive oil

4 large leeks, chopped

1 large onion, chopped

1 1/2 pounds carrots, peeled and cut into 1/2-inch pieces

4 cups chicken broth

1 tablespoon fresh thyme

1 bay leaf

salt and freshly ground pepper to taste

1 12-ounce can evaporated milk

freshly grated nutmeg, for serving

In a soup pot, heat the oil over medium-high heat. When it is hot, add the leeks and onion, and sauté until soft. Add the carrots, broth, 2 cups water, and the seasonings, and bring to a boil. Reduce the heat, cover, and let simmer until the vegetables are tender, about 40 minutes. Remove from heat, discard the bay leaf, and let cool slightly. Pass through a food mill, or purée in a blender. Return the soup to the pot, and stir in the milk over medium heat. Heat just to scalding. Sprinkle nutmeg over each serving, and serve at once.

This soup can be varied by substituting some of the carrots with parsnips or butternut squash.

Chicken Senegalese Soup

Serves 3 to 4

1 10 3/4-ounce can condensed cream
    of chicken soup
1 can (12-ounce) milk
juice of 1 lemon (or to taste)
1 teaspoon curry powder (or to taste)
sour cream, for serving

In a blender, combine the soup, milk, lemon juice and curry powder. Blend well. Serve chilled, and garnish with a dollop of sour cream.

Quick and Easy Vegetable Soup

Serves 6 to 8

2 tablespoons vegetable oil

1 large onion, chopped

1 teaspoon minced garlic

1 cup celery, sliced

1 cup carrots, chopped or sliced

2 cans (14 1/2-ounces each) vegetable broth

1 15-ounce package frozen, cut green beans

2 cups chicken broth or water

2 teaspoons dry basil leaves

1 tablespoon Mrs. Dash (garlic and herb flavor)

1 medium zucchini, quartered and sliced thinly

1 15-ounce can crushed tomatoes

In a 3-quart soup pot, sauté onion in oil over medium-high heat for about one minute, until softened. Add garlic, celery, and carrots, and sauté about one minute. Add vegetable broth and beans. Bring to a boil. Add chicken broth, basil, Mrs. Dash and zucchini. Reduce heat, and let simmer for 20 to 30 minutes, until carrots are tender. Add crushed tomatoes.

Serve as a main course with your favorite crusty bread, or as a first course.

What could be cozier in front of warm hearth than a bowl of hot soup, this is quick, easy and healthful.

Portuguese Onion Soup

Created by Chef Michael Hamm, Sr. of Whitney's Inn
Serves 12

1/2 cup (8 tablespoons) butter

2 large Bermuda onions, chopped

1 clove garlic, minced

2 tablespoons commercially prepared beef base, or 4 bouillon cubes dissolved in 2 tablespoons boiling water

freshly ground pepper to taste

10 ounces red wine, Merlot or Cabernet Sauvignon

12 slices crusty, rustic bread

12 1-ounce slices Provolone cheese

For the garnish:

paprika

thinly sliced scallions

In a large soup pot, melt the butter over medium-high heat. When it is hot, stir in the onion, garlic, beef base, and pepper, and bring to a boil. Add the wine, and bring back to a boil. Add 3 quarts water, reduce the heat to medium, and let simmer for at least 30 minutes. Preheat oven to 375 degrees. Ladle the soup into oven safe-bowls. Top each portion with a slice of bread, then with a slice of cheese. Bake until the cheese melts, and is golden brown. Sprinkle with paprika and scallions, and serve at once.

Potato Leek Soup
Serves 4 to 6
(makes about 2 1/2 quarts)

3 tablespoons butter

4 or 5 medium leeks, well washed of sand, white part only, chopped

2 or 3 medium white onions, chopped

4 cups chicken broth, plus additional broth as needed for thinning

4 medium white potatoes, peeled and chopped

salt and freshly ground pepper

parsley for serving

In a large soup pot, melt the butter over medium-high heat. Add the leeks and onions, and sauté for 5 minutes, being careful not to brown them. Add the broth and potatoes, and let simmer for 45 minutes.

Purée the mixture by batches in a blender. If the resulting soup is too thick, add more broth to thin it as desired. Season to taste, and serve hot.

Garnish with parsley, and serve with French bread.

Woodbine Tomato Soup

Serves 6 to 8 (makes about 2 quarts)

8 pounds tomatoes, cored and
 quartered

2 stalks celery, chopped

5 whole cloves

1 bay leaf

1 cup parsley sprigs

1/4 cup (4 tablespoons) butter

4 tablespoons flour

1 tablespoon sugar

3 teaspoons salt

For the garnish:
unsweetened whipped cream
ground cloves
basil leaves

In a soup kettle, combine the tomatoes, celery, cloves, bay leaf, and parsley over medium-high heat. When the mixture just comes to a boil, reduce heat and let simmer for 2 hours.

In a small saucepan, melt the butter over medium-high heat. Add the flour, and whisk until smooth. Cook for about 1 minute, whisking constantly, until foamy. Remove from heat.

Strain the soup into a clean pot. Whisk the butter and flour mixture into the soup until smooth. Add the sugar and salt, and heat until hot. Serve with a dollop of whipped cream, cloves and basil.

Farmstand Tomato Soup

Makes 5 cups

4 large tomatoes (about 2 pounds), cored, cut in half crosswise, and seeded

3 teaspoons olive oil

1 cup chopped carrot

2 garlic cloves, chopped

1 tablespoon chopped fresh basil or oregano, plus more for garnish

1 teaspoon chopped fresh thyme, plus more for garnish

1 16-ounce can fat-free, reduced-sodium chicken broth

1 cup 1% reduced-fat milk

1/4 teaspoon salt

1/4 teaspoon freshly ground pepper

Preheat oven to 425 degrees. Place the tomato halves, cut-side down, on a jelly-roll pan, and drizzle with 2 teaspoons of the oil. Bake for 35 minutes, until tender and slightly charred. Remove tomatoes from oven, let cool. Discard tomato skins.

Heat the remaining 1 teaspoon oil in a 2-quart saucepan over medium-high heat. Add the carrot, garlic, and herbs. Sauté for 8 minutes. Stir in the broth. Partially cover, reduce the heat, and let simmer for 20 minutes, or until the carrots are tender. Add the tomato halves. Place half of the mixture in a blender, and process until smooth. Repeat with the remaining mixture. Return the puréed mixture to pan. Add the milk, salt and pepper, and stir over low heat until thoroughly heated. Do not boil. Sprinkle with additional fresh herbs just before serving.

Cream of Pumpkin and Apple Soup

Courtesy of Spring Ledge Farm

Serves 4 to 6

2 tablespoons butter

2/3 cup chopped celery

2/3 cup chopped onion

3 cups peeled pumpkin or winter
squash chunks

1 1/2 cups peeled apple chunks

3 cups chicken broth

1/2 cup instant rice (uncooked)

1 cup light cream or evaporated milk

salt to taste

1/2 teaspoon curry powder

freshly grated nutmeg, for serving

In a soup pot, melt the butter over medium-high heat. When it is hot, add the celery and onion, and sauté until soft. Add the pumpkin, apple, broth, 1/2 cup water and rice, and bring to a boil. Reduce the heat, cover, and let simmer until the pumpkin and apples are very soft (20 to 30 minutes).

Remove from heat, and pass through a food mill or purée in a blender. Pour the soup into a clean pot, and stir in the milk, salt and curry powder over medium heat. Heat just to scalding. Sprinkle nutmeg on each serving, and serve at once.

Gap Mountain Stew

Created by Chef Devin Ells of The Inn at East Hill Farm

Serves 8 to 12

1 cup diced carrots

1 cup diced celery

1 cup diced bell peppers

1 cup diced onions

1 teaspoon minced garlic

1/4 cup commercially prepared vegetable stock base or 4 bouillon cubes

1 cup tomato paste

1 teaspoon Cajun seasoning

1 teaspoon salt-free herb seasoning

2 cups cooked macaroni

In a 4-quart saucepan, sauté the carrots, celery, peppers, onions, and garlic over medium heat for 15 to 20 minutes, until lightly browned. Add 2 quarts water and the vegetable stock base. Bring to a boil, and whisk in the tomato paste and seasonings. Reduce the heat to medium-low, and let simmer for 30 minutes. Add the macaroni, and serve.

Roasted Red Pepper Eggplant Soup
Serves 4 (10-onnce servings)

1 1/2 pounds eggplant

2 red bell peppers

3 cups fat-free, low-sodium chicken
   broth (preferably homemade)

1 1/2 cups chopped yellow onion

1/2 teaspoon salt

1/8 teaspoon freshly ground pepper

For the garnish:

1/4 cup sliced fresh basil

Preheat broiler. Cut the eggplant and peppers in half lengthwise. Place skin-side up on a foil-lined baking sheet, and broil for 15 minutes, until blackened. Transfer the peppers to a zip-lock plastic bag, close tightly, and let stand for 10 minutes. Peel the peppers, and discard the skin and membrane. Remove the seeds from the eggplant, scoop the pulp into a small bowl, and discard the skin and seeds. Reserve the eggplant pulp and peeled peppers. In a medium saucepan, combine 1 cup of the broth and the onion over medium-high heat. Bring to a boil, reduce the heat, and let simmer for 5 minutes. Stir in the remaining 2 cups of broth, and the peppers and eggplant pulp, and let simmer for 10 minutes. Transfer the mixture to a blender, and blend until smooth. Return the puréed mixture to the saucepan. Stir in the salt and pepper, and heat until hot. Garnish with basil, and serve at once.

"I have found leaving the membrane and seeds on the red bell pepper, and the seeds in the eggplant while broiling adds flavor. Quick, easy and very good."
-*Natalie Harrington Zook*

Crab and Asparagus Soup

Created by Executive Chef Jeffrey Woolley of The Manor On Golden Pond
Serves 8 (10-ounce servings)

1 bunch asparagus

2 quarts chicken broth

10 ounces lump crabmeat picked over for cartilage

6 ounces baby spinach

salt and freshly ground pepper to taste

Trim and discard the dry ends from the asparagus, and cut the tips into 2-to 3-inch pieces (reserve). Chop the remaining stems. In a soup pot, combine the broth and asparagus stems over medium-high heat. Bring to a boil, reduce the heat, cover, and let simmer for 30 minutes.

Strain the chopped stems from the broth. Return the broth to the stove over medium heat. Add the crabmeat, spinach, and reserved asparagus tips, and let simmer for 10 minutes. Season with salt and pepper.

"This recipe was the brainchild of our dining room manager, Mark Reeder, trying to assist me in menu planning. After much trial and error, we developed this simple soup."

Sunset Hill House

Spectacular mountain views

Since 1880, guests of this historic Second Empire Grand Hotel legacy have been enjoying premium service and spectacular mountain views. The view from the Inn's dining room windows was chosen by Yankee Magazine as the centerfold picture for the article "Best Views with a Room" in October, 1999. Our Executive Chef Joseph Peterson, a Johnson & Wales graduate, has been featured in Bon Appetit and Gourmet magazines. At Sunset Hill House, you will enjoy fabulous sunrises and sunsets, superb food and a casual tavern. Some of the twenty-eight rooms feature fireplaces, Jacuzzis, suites and porches. The facilities include on-premise golf, a heated pool, cross-country skiing, hiking and beautiful gardens. The Inn can also accommodate weddings, reunions and conference functions.

Sunset Hill House
231 Sunset Hill Road
Sugar Hill, NH 03585
603.823.5522
800.786.4455
www.sunsethillhouse.com
Innkeepers Nancy and Lon Henderson

Grilled Seafood Soup

Created by Executive Chef Joseph Peterson of Sunset Hill House
Serves 4

For the broth:

1 medium potato, well scrubbed

1 medium onion, coarsely chopped

3 ounces Portuguese sausage
   (Linguica)

1 hot cherry pepper (Pastene brand,
   if possible)

1 1/4 cups brown ale

12 clams in the shell, well scrubbed

salt and freshly ground pepper to
   taste

12 sea scallops, shucked

12 large shrimp, shelled

12 mussels, in the shell

For the garnish:

1 tablespoon sliced scallions

1 tablespoon diced red bell pepper

1 tablespoon minced parsley

In a 4-quart pot, combine the potato, onion, sausage, pepper, ale, and 2 cups water over high heat. Bring to a boil, lower the heat, and let simmer until the potato is tender. Add the clams, salt and pepper, and cover tightly. Simmer until the clams open. Remove from heat; reserve the clams, and strain and reserve the broth.

Grill the scallops and shrimp over high heat until just cooked. Steam the mussels (or grill them, covered) until they open.

In a serving bowl, arrange the shellfish. Garnish. Bring the reserved broth to a simmer. Bring the serving dish to the table, pour the hot broth over the arranged seafood, and enjoy!

This wonderfully flavorful soup has a unique presentation, sure to entertain and impress your guests!

Lobster Chowda' with Smoked Bacon

Created by Executive Chef Jeffrey Woolley of The Manor On Golden Pond
Serves 8 (10-ounce servings)

1 tablespoon butter

1/2 pound applewood smoked bacon, diced

1 small onion, diced

6 tablespoons flour

32 ounces clam juice

2 cups milk

3/4 pound lobster meat, diced

2 teaspoons celery seed

2 tablespoons chopped parsley

salt and freshly ground pepper, to taste

1 cup heavy cream

In a soup pot, melt the butter over medium heat. Add the bacon and onion, and sauté until golden brown. Stir in the flour, and cook for a moment. Add the clam juice and milk, and bring to a boil, stirring occasionally. Reduce the heat to a simmer. Add the lobster, celery seed, parsley, salt and pepper. After a few minutes, when the lobster is cooked, stir in the cream, and heat until scalding. Serve at once.

"While honeymooning in Nantucket, I stopped at a walk-up fish shop and got a bowl of seafood chowder. The smoked bacon gave a wonderful flavor, and compensated for the lack of filler potatoes. This is my version."

Smoked Trout, Sweet Potato **and** Corn Chowder

Created by Chef John Riccelli of The Inn on Newfound Lake

Serves 8 to 10

3 strips bacon

1/2 cup diced white onions

2 cups native Silver Queen corn (or any other sweet corn) kernels (about 5 ears), cobs reserved

6 cups chicken stock

1 1/2 tablespoons minced fresh thyme

2 cups flaked, smoked trout

3 tablespoons cornstarch

1 1/2 cups cooked sweet potatoes, cut into 3/4-inch cubes

1 1/4 cups heavy cream

salt and freshly ground pepper

1 1/2 tablespoons chopped scallions, for serving

In a large soup pot, cook the bacon and onions over medium heat until the onions are translucent, 4 to 5 minutes. With a slotted spoon, remove and discard the bacon. Add both the corn kernels and cobs to the soup pot, and stir in the stock and thyme. Bring to a boil, reduce the heat, and let simmer for 10 minutes. Add the smoked trout, and simmer for 2 minutes. Remove and discard the corncobs. Dissolve the cornstarch in 3 tablespoons cold water, and slowly add to the chowder. Bring it back to a boil, and let boil for 2 minutes, stirring carefully. Reduce the heat to low. Add the sweet potatoes, cream, and salt and pepper to taste. Cook, stirring occasionally, for 2 minutes. Sprinkle the scallions over the chowder, and serve at once.

"Here on Newfound Lake, on the threshold of the White Mountains, smoked rainbow trout and native 'Silver Queen' corn seem to be natural choices for this chowder."

Quick Corn Chowder

Serves 4

1 medium onion, chopped
2 tablespoons butter
1 teaspoon sugar
1 teaspoon salt
2 tablespoons flour
1/4 teaspoon freshly ground pepper
1 15-ounce can cream-style corn
2 cups milk, scalded
2 cups boiling water
1 egg yolk, lightly beaten

In a 2-quart saucepan, sauté the onion in the butter over medium-high heat until soft. Sprinkle in the sugar, salt, flour and pepper, and continue cooking for a few moments, until mixture thickens. Reduce heat to medium, and stir in the corn thoroughly. Stir in the milk and water, and reduce heat to medium-low. Cook, stirring occasionally, until thickened, about 30 minutes. Just before serving, remove from heat, add the egg yolk, and whisk vigorously for about 1 minute.

Corn Chowder
Serves 8

6 slices bacon, cut into 1/2-inch pieces

1 onion, coarsely chopped

1 fennel bulb, coarsely chopped

2 to 4 cloves garlic, crushed

4 tablespoons flour

4 cups chicken broth

4 large Yukon Gold potatoes, coarsely chopped

2 cups frozen and thawed corn kernels, or kernels cut from ears of fresh corn

3 tablespoons rice wine vinegar (or to taste)

pinch of kosher salt

freshly ground pepper to taste

1 cup heavy cream

In a large soup pot over medium-high heat, brown the bacon for 5 minutes. Add the onion, fennel and garlic, and sauté for 2 minutes. Sprinkle in the flour, and stir over the heat for 4 minutes. Slowly add the broth, whisking constantly. Add the potatoes, and cook until tender, about 20 minutes. Add the remaining ingredients except the cream, and heat until hot. Just before serving, add the cream; do not let boil.

"Adapted from a TV recipe I found when I first moved to New Hampshire in 1997. This can be made one day ahead, adding the cream at the last minute. Chop the vegetables in large chunks, as it is a chowder." - *Karen Barnhart*

Mom's Beef Stew
Serves 4 to 6

1 1/2 pounds beef, top sirloin or chuck, cut into 2-inch pieces

1 tablespoon salt

1/4 teaspoon freshly ground pepper

flour, for coating the beef

6 tablespoons vegetable oil

4 beef bouillon cubes

1 1/2 teaspoons dried thyme

3 tablespoons ketchup

1 1/2 tablespoons Worcestershire sauce

1 bay leaf

4 all-purpose potatoes

1 onion

3 carrots

Season the meat with the salt and pepper, and toss it with flour to coat. In a 4-quart saucepan, heat the oil over medium-high heat until hot. Add the meat, and brown thoroughly. Add 3 cups water, the bouillon, thyme, ketchup, Worcestershire sauce and bay leaf. Cover, reduce heat, and let simmer for 1 1/2 hours; add more water as necessary.

Trim and peel the vegetables, and cut them into large chunks. Add them to the stew, stir thoroughly, cover, and continue cooking for 1 hour longer. Remove bay leaf before serving.

"Mom's recipe — perfect for winter weekends. If you let it simmer all day, the meat will be especially tender." - *Melisa Weber*

Winter Beef Stew

Serves 6 to 8

2 tablespoons vegetable oil

2 pounds stew beef, cut into 1-inch pieces

3 cups strong coffee

4 tablespoons molasses

2 cloves garlic, minced

1 teaspoon salt

2 teaspoons Worcestershire sauce

1 teaspoon dried oregano

4 carrots, sliced 1/2 inch thick

4 small onions, quartered

4 medium potatoes, diced

6 tablespoons flour

In a large soup pot, heat the oil over medium-high heat until hot. Add the meat, and brown it thoroughly. Add the coffee, molasses, garlic, salt, Worcestershire sauce, and oregano, and stir to combine well. Cover, reduce heat, and let simmer for 1 1/2 hours.

Add 3 cups water and the vegetables, and let simmer, uncovered, until vegetables are tender, about 30 minutes. In a small bowl, stir the flour into 1/2 cup cold water until no lumps remain; stir this into the stew. Cook, stirring frequently, until the stew has thickened, and is piping hot.

French Oven Beef Stew

Serves 4 to 6

2 pounds stew beef

2 stalks celery, coarsely chopped

1 1/2 cups tomato juice or V-8 juice,
    plus additional juice as needed

1/2 teaspoon salt

1/2 teaspoon dried basil

2 medium onions, coarsely chopped

1/3 cup quick-cooking tapioca

1 teaspoon sugar

1/4 teaspoon freshly ground pepper

4 medium potatoes, pared and cut
    into large chunks

Preheat oven to 300 degrees.
In a 2 1/2-quart casserole, combine all
the ingredients except the potatoes.
Cover tightly, and bake for 2 1/2
hours. Add the potatoes and cook,
uncovered, 1 hour longer, stirring
occasionally. If the stew seems too
thick, thin it with more tomato juice.

Salads, Vegetables, Sauces & Condiments

Town Pound

Town Pound

Wandering animals were a hazard to farmers' fields, inflicting major damage to crops. Early on in Hopkinton's history, this issue was raised at Town Meeting numerous times. The answer to the problem was a pound, which would be used to hold animals found loose in the town and a fee was required from the owners to get their animals out again.

As early as 1767, the town voted to build a pound behind the meetinghouse, thirty feet square and eight feet high. In 1773, it was decided that hogs might run at large, "if yoaked and Ringed." In 1792, citizens voted "to build a pound on Captain Thomas Bailey's land, nigh where his old house stood, said pound to be 30 feet square within, 8 feet high, and built with round pine logs, the gate and its posts to be of white oak, the hinges of iron, and provided with a good lock."

In 1798, the issue was further clarified: "Domestic animals were prohibited from running at large within a half mile of the town-house, under penalty of 1 dollar for a swine, twenty-five cents for a sheep, and $1.25 for a neat creature unless it should appear that the estray was by accident."

In 1805, voters decided to purchase land and build a pound "within a reasonable distance from the center of the town." Built of stones, this pound still stands on old Putney Hill Road as pictured. Finally, in 1878 the town voted to build pounds for people called "tramp-houses." (One was adjacent to this animal pound.) There vagrants were provided with bread, water, and a night's lodging, with the proviso that they leave town in the morning.

AUDREY GARDNER

Even as a small child, Audrey Gardner loved to draw. She studied at the School of the Museum of Fine Arts, in Boston, and was awarded a teaching degree from Tufts University. She loves working with children, and she has taught art at several schools, most recently in Massachusetts. Currently she has begun to study watercolor, which she finds challenging, but intriguing.

Curried Fruit and Nut Salad

Serves 8

For the salad:

1 head red-leaf lettuce, washed and torn into bite-size pieces

1 1/2 cups fresh spinach, washed, stems removed, and torn into bite-size pieces

1 11-ounce can Mandarin orange sections, chilled and drained

1 1/2 cups seedless purple grapes, halved

For the dressing:

1/2 cup extra-virgin olive oil

1/3 cup balsamic vinegar

1 clove garlic, minced

2 tablespoons brown sugar

2 tablespoons minced chives

1 tablespoon curry powder

1 teaspoon soy sauce

For serving:

1/4 cup slivered almonds

1 avocado, peeled and sliced

In a serving bowl, toss together the salad ingredients. In a jar with a tight-fitting lid, shake together the dressing ingredients until well blended. Dress the salad, and scatter over the almonds and avocado.

Spinach Salad

Serves 10 to 12

For the salad:

1 pound fresh spinach, washed, stems removed, and torn into bite-size pieces

1/2 cup chopped walnuts

3/4 cup dried cranberries

For the dressing:

2/3 cup extra-virgin olive oil

1/3 cup balsamic vinegar

1 clove garlic, minced

3/4 tablespoon Kosher salt

1/2 teaspoon coarsely ground pepper

In a serving bowl, toss together the salad ingredients. In a jar with a tight-fitting lid, shake together the dressing ingredients until well blended. Dress the salad, and serve.

"A previous version of this recipe was given to me more than 30 years ago, and that version I shared in the St. Andrew's Cookbook. Over the years I've adapted the recipe for health purposes." *-Karen Dufault*

Mandarin Orange Salad with Poppy Seed Dressing

Serves 4 to 6

For the salad:

1 head Romaine lettuce, torn into small pieces

1/2 cup slivered almonds, toasted until golden brown

1 11-ounce can Mandarin orange sections, drained

For the dressing:

1/2 cup sugar

2/3 cup vegetable oil

1 teaspoon prepared mustard

1 tablespoon poppy seeds

1/4 cup vinegar

1 teaspoon salt

In a serving bowl, toss togather the salad ingredients. In a small, microwave-safe bowl, whisk together the dressing ingredients. Warm in a microwave oven for 1 minute. Pour the desired amount of dressing over the salad. Toss to combine well, and serve at once.

Seared Duck Salad

Created by Chef Glenn Gonyea of the Chesterfield Inn
Serves 6

For the salad:

3 whole 12–14-ounce duck breasts

1 tablespoon olive oil

1 tablespoon minced fresh rosemary

2 tablespoons minced garlic

salt and freshly ground pepper to taste

1 pound baby spinach

For the dressing:

2 cups olive oil

1/4 cup Champagne vinegar

1 tablespoon capers

1/4 cup balsamic vinegar

1/4 cup sundried tomatoes packed in oil, julienned

1 cup crumbled Gorgonzola cheese

1 tablespoon chopped fresh basil

2 tablespoons prepared horseradish

1 tablespoon Dijon mustard

2 teaspoons chopped fresh ginger

1 tablespoon minced shallots

Prepare the duck:

Split the duck breasts, rinse under cold, running water, and pat dry. In a large, nonstick skillet, warm the olive oil over medium-low heat. Add the duck, skin-side down. Sprinkle with rosemary, garlic, salt and pepper. Cook for about 5 minutes, until the skin is crisp and brown. Turn the duck over, and cook for 10 to 15 minutes longer, to desired doneness.

Prepare the dressing:

Whisk together the dressing ingredients until well combined.

Assemble the salad:

Toss the spinach with the desired amount of dressing, and divide among 6 serving plates. Slice each half duck breast across the width into 5 or 6 slices, and fan the slices across each serving of salad. Spoon additional dressing over the sliced duck, if desired, and serve at once.

Boston Seaside Salad

Serves 6

For the dressing:

1 clove garlic, minced

1/2 teaspoon salt

1/8 teaspoon freshly ground pepper

1/2 teaspoon dry mustard

1 teaspoon Worcestershire sauce

2 scallions, finely chopped

1 cup mayonnaise

1/2 cup sour cream

For the salad:

1 head Boston lettuce, torn into small pieces

1/2 head leaf lettuce or Romaine, torn into small pieces

1/2 cup minced parsley

1 cup halved cherry or grape tomatoes

1 cup medium shrimp, cooked and peeled

Combine the dressing ingredients, and refrigerate. In a serving bowl, toss the salad ingredients. Pour the desired amount of dressing over the assembled salad, toss to combine well, and serve at once.

This dressing may be prepared the day before. It is great for salad or for dipping. Light mayonnaise and no-fat sour cream may be used. The dressing may be thinned with milk.

Spicy Slaw
Serves 10

1/4 cup sugar

1/4 cup rice or cider vinegar

1/2 teaspoon salt

2 teaspoons freshly ground pepper

3/4 cup vegetable oil

1/4 cup dark sesame oil

1 1/2 tablespoons hot chili oil

1 small head (2 1/4 pounds) cabbage, finely shredded (use slicer on food processor)

1 cup chopped green onion

3 3-ounce packages Oriental noodles with seasoning mix

1 cup slivered almonds, toasted

1/4 cup sesame seeds, toasted

To make the dressing, combine the sugar, vinegar, salt and pepper in a medium bowl, and whisk until the sugar dissolves. Whisk in the oils until well blended. In a large bowl, toss together the cabbage and green onion. Add the dressing, and mix well. Cover tightly and refrigerate overnight (mixture will wilt and decrease in volume).

Six hours before serving, crumble the uncooked noodles over the cabbage mixture. Sprinkle with the seasoning (from the packets) and toss to mix well. Cover tightly, and refrigerate. (Noodles will soften.) Just before serving, add the almonds and sesame seeds, and toss to combine.

Corned Beef Salad Mold

Serves 10

1 3 1/2-ounce package lemon Jello
2 tablespoons vinegar
1 cup boiling water
1 can (12 ounces) corned beef, crumbled
1 small onion, diced
2 stalks celery, diced
1 medium green bell pepper, diced
1 cup mayonnaise
1 tablespoon prepared horseradish
3 hard-cooked eggs, diced

In a medium bowl, combine the Jello and vinegar with the boiling water, and stir until the Jello has dissolved. Refrigerate for 30 to 60 minutes, until it is thick and beginning to set. Fold in the remaining ingredients thoroughly. Grease a 1-quart mold, and fill it with the gelatin mixture. Cover tightly, and refrigerate until set.

"This recipe was given to me by Ann McCann of the Bucksport (Maine) Golf Club, when the lady golfers of the Castine Golf Club visited Bucksport for a match and lunch. It is easy to fix, and is a nice lunch or brunch salad."
- *Mary Jane Miller*

Corn Casserole

Serves 6 to 8

Low-fat version:

2 cups frozen corn kernels, thawed

4 tablespoons low-fat margarine

1/2 cup egg substitute

1/4 cup cornmeal

1 cup low-fat sour cream

1 cup diced low-fat jalapeno Jack cheese

1 teaspoon salt

Regular version:

2 cups frozen corn kernels, thawed

1/4 cup (4 tablespoons) butter, melted

2 eggs

1/4 cup cornmeal

1 cup sour cream

1 cup diced jalapeno Jack cheese, plus additional cheese for topping, if desired

1 teaspoon salt

Preheat oven to 350 degrees. In a small bowl, toss the corn with the butter. In a medium mixing bowl, beat the eggs well. Add the cornmeal, sour cream, cheese and salt, and mix well. Stir the corn thoroughly into the egg mixture. Pour into a 2-quart casserole. Top with additional cheese if desired, and bake for 45 to 60 minutes, until bubbly.

The Yankee Theory of Relativity

"How you doing, Ezra," Royal asks.

"Pretty good, considering what I've been through."

"What's that?" Sympathetically.

"Well, the last thing was a set of stairs."

Corn and Chive Pudding

Serves 8

2 10-ounce packages frozen corn kernels, thawed

1/4 cup sugar

1 1/4 teaspoons salt

2 cups milk

4 eggs

1/2 vanilla bean, split lengthwise and seeds scraped, pod reserved for another use

1/4 cup (4 tablespoons) unsalted butter, melted and cooled

3 tablespoons flour

1/4 cup chopped fresh chives

pinch of freshly grated nutmeg

For the garnish:

3 tablespoons minced fresh chives

Preheat oven to 325 degrees. Butter a 1 1/2-quart quiche dish or pie plate. In a food processor fitted with the steel blade, process half of the corn until it is coarsely chopped. In a medium bowl, stir together the chopped corn and the remaining corn kernels, and sprinkle with the sugar and salt, stirring to combine well.

In another medium bowl, whisk together the milk, eggs, vanilla seeds, butter, flour and chives. Add this mixture to the corn mixture, and stir until well combined. Pour the pudding mixture into the prepared pan, and sprinkle with nutmeg. Bake in the middle of the oven until the pudding's center is just set, about 40 to 45 minutes. Garnish with chives.

Scalloped Tomatoes
Serves 4 to 6

3 tablespoons butter

1 medium onion, thinly sliced

1 18-ounce can whole tomatoes

2 slices white bread, cut into small
pieces

3 tablespoons flour

1 green bell pepper, trimmed,
blanched, and thinly sliced

sugar, salt and freshly ground pepper

1/4 cup breadcrumbs for topping

Preheat oven to 350 degrees. Butter a 1 1/2- to 2-quart baking dish. In a heavy soup pot, melt the butter over medium-high heat. Add the onion, and sauté until soft. Add the tomatoes and bread, and stir. Sprinkle with the flour, and stir well. Cook until fairly thick, and no longer soupy, about 15 to 20 minutes. Stir in the bell pepper, and season to taste with sugar, salt and pepper. Pour the mixture into the prepared dish and sprinkle with breadcrumbs. Bake for 15 to 20 minutes, until the crumb topping is golden brown.

Variation: Stir 1 cup cooked snap beans into the tomato mixture, and add 1/4 teaspoon prepared mustard and 1/4 cup grated cheese to the topping mixture.

Sweet Potato Hash

Created by Chef John Riccelli of The Inn on Newfound Lake

Serves 4

1 1/2 tablespoons olive oil

1 cup thinly sliced white onions

2 tablespoons cold butter

1/3 cup dried cranberries

2 cups cooked sweet potatoes, cut into 3/4-inch cubes

1 tablespoon Dijon mustard

2 tablespoons chopped scallions

salt and freshly ground pepper to taste

Warm the oil in a large skillet over medium heat. When it is hot, add the onions, and sauté until translucent, about 5 minutes. Drain off excess oil. Add the cold butter, cranberries and sweet potatoes, and cook for 4 to 5 minutes without stirring, so the potatoes brown. Stir, scraping the bottom of the pan. Stir in the mustard, scallions, and salt and pepper. Cook for 5 to 10 minutes longer, stirring occasionally; do not overstir. When the potatoes are lightly browned and crisp, serve at once.

"Rustic and homey! I love this dish any time of the year. Served at the inn with Grilled Duck (recipe on page 126)".

Riverview Farms Inn

A nice place to ...

Riverview Farms Inn is ideally located in the quaint New England village of Wilmot Flat, New Hampshire. The Inn features beautiful suites with private living rooms and kitchenettes, and wonderful sun decks overlooking the river. The Inn is within easy traveling distance to several New England areas, including the old New England charm of Dartmouth College in Hanover; the town of New London with its great tax-free shops; Queechee, Vermont with its scenic gorge; Woodstock, Vermont, with its wonderful historic sites; and Concord, New Hampshire, the state's capital. The area surrounding the Inn also has wonderful restaurants, plus lakes for swimming and boating, and hiking, biking, theatre and arts. If your stay is during the winter months, the Inn is conveniently located between two major ski areas, Mt. Sunapee and Ragged Mountain. The Inn is also situated between the prestigious private prep school Proctor Academy and Colby-Sawyer College, a fine co-ed college with a lovely campus.

Riverview Farms Inn
1 Village Road
Wilmot, NH 03287
603.526.4482
800.392.9627
www.newlondon-nh.com
Owner M. Pacetta

Sweet Potato Pie

Created by M. Pacetta of Riverview Farms Inn
Serves 8

For the potatoes:

6 pounds sweet potatoes, baked until tender and skinned

1/3 cup (packed) light brown sugar

1/2 cup (8 tablespoons) butter, softened

3 eggs, beaten

1 teaspoon vanilla extract

3 tablespoons dark rum

1 teaspoon pumpkin pie spice

1/3 cup evaporated milk

For the topping:

1/4 cup (4 tablespoons) butter

1/4 cup (packed) light brown sugar

1/4 cup flour

3/4 cup chopped pecans

Preheat oven to 350 degrees.

Prepare the potatoes:

In a large bowl, mash the potatoes. Add the remaining ingredients (except for the topping ingredients), and combine thoroughly. Generously butter a 13 x 9 x 2-inch Pyrex baking dish, and evenly spread the potato mixture in the dish. (At this point, the potato mixture can be refrigerated, tightly covered, until needed.)

Prepare the topping:

In a small saucepan, melt the butter over medium-high heat. Add the remaining ingredients, and stir to combine well. Spread evenly over the potato mixture, and bake for 35 minutes, until bubbly.

French Mashed Potatoes

Created by Executive Chef Joseph Peterson of the Sunset Hill House
Serves 6

2 pounds Red Bliss potatoes, peeled if desired

3/4 cup (12 tablespoons) butter, soffened

1 tablespoon prepared horseradish

3 ounces sour cream

Freshly ground pepper to taste

In a large saucepan, boil the potatoes in lightly salted water until tender. Drain, and place in a large mixing bowl. Add the butter, horse-radish, sour cream and pepper. Beat until well blended. Serve at once.

"Once your guests taste these mashed potatoes, the recipe will become a standard in your household."

Browned Potatoes

Created by Dennis and Roberta Aufranc at Maple Hill Farm

Serves 4

Olive oil, for sautéing

1 clove garlic, minced

4 medium potatoes, cooked and sliced 1/2 inch thick

salt and freshly ground pepper to taste

minced fresh basil to taste

Cover the bottom of a large sauté pan with a film of oil. Over medium-high heat, warm the pan. When it is hot, add the garlic, and sauté for about 1 minute, to give the oil flavor. Add the potatoes, and season with salt, pepper and basil. Sauté until the potatoes are brown on both sides. Serve hot.

Browned Potatoes are a great accompaniment to the Loin of Pork found on page 142.

Maple Salad Dressing

Makes 1 1/2 cups

1 cup vegetable oil
1/3 cup cider vinegar
3 tablespoons maple syrup
1 1/2 teaspoons salt
1/2 teaspoon freshly ground pepper
1/2 teaspoon dry mustard
1 clove garlic, minced

Combine all ingredients in a pint jar, cover tightly, and shake until thoroughly combined.

Jay's Vinaigrette

Created by Chef Laurie Tweedie of The Darby Field Inn & Restaurant
Serves 2 to 4

1 cup cider vinegar
2 cups soybean, canola, or other neutral oil
1 large onion, coarsely chopped
3 cloves garlic
1 tablespoon freshly ground pepper
2 tablespoons salt
3 tablespoons sugar
1 teaspoon dried dill weed

Put all the ingredients in a blender, and blend on high speed until smooth and emulsified. Serve with any type of green salad.

Sunshine Mango Salsa

Makes about 2 cups

1/4 cup lime juice

1 cup canned pineapple juice

1/4 cup red-wine vinegar

1 teaspoon minced garlic

1 tablespoon chopped cilantro

1 tablespoon curry powder

salt and freshly ground pepper to taste

3 ripe mangoes, peeled and diced

1 small red bell pepper, seeded and diced

1 small green bell pepper, seeded and diced

1 small red onion, sliced

In a medium bowl, combine the lime juice, pineapple juice, vinegar, garlic, cilantro, curry powder, salt and pepper. Add the remaining ingredients, and fold gently to combine thoroughly. Cover tightly, and refrigerate up to 3 days.

Perfect Pesto

Makes 2 cups

1 cup walnuts

4 to 6 large cloves garlic

2 cups (lightly packed) fresh basil

1 cup olive oil

1 cup freshly grated Parmesan
cheese

1/4 cup freshly grated Romano
cheese

salt and freshly ground pepper
to taste

In the workbowl of a food processor fitted with the steel blade, process the walnuts and garlic until very finely chopped or pasty. Add the basil, half of the oil, and the cheeses, and process until smooth. Add more oil as necessary to achieve a smooth consistency. Season with salt and pepper.

To freeze, pour pesto into an airtight container, sprinkling the surface with more cheese, and then covering with a film of olive oil.

Pesto can be used on pasta, meat or as a chip dip. It's very strong and may be an acquired taste.

Cranberry-Orange Relish

Created by Chef Tracy Foor of the Mountain Lake Inn

2 pounds cranberries

2 oranges, well scrubbed, quartered and seeded

4 stalks celery, trimmed

2 cups crushed pineapple

4 cups sugar

In the workbowl of a food processor fitted with the steel blade, separately grind the cranberries, oranges and celery; scrape each into a large bowl when ground. Stir in the pineapple and sugar thoroughly. Cover tightly, and refrigerate overnight.

"My mother would serve this every Thanksgiving, Christmas and Easter. It is certainly a hit at holiday time."

Quick and Perfect Blender Hollandaise

Created by Chef Ann Carlsmith of the Stepping Stones Bed & Breakfast
Makes 1 1/2 cups

2 egg yolks

2 tablespoons boiling water

1 cup (16 tablespoons) butter, melted
and kept at a boil

juice of 1 lemon

salt and freshly ground pepper to
taste

fresh herbs such as chives or basil to
taste

In a blender container, blend the egg yolks on high speed until light. With the motor running, slowly dribble in the boiling water, then the boiling butter. It is important that both water and butter be very hot, to cook and thicken the yolks; add them slowly to avoid curdling. Add the lemon juice, salt and pepper, and blend. Add minced herbs to flavor the sauce, or use whole leaves as a garnish.

"This recipe has often been requested by guests. It is fool-proof and quickly done. Refrigerate extra sauce. Gently rewarmed and thinned with heavy cream, it makes a superb, delicate fish sauce, too."

Pasta, Grains, Beans & Cheese

French's Home and Hearth

French's Home and Hearth

This home was built in 1760 by Abraham Kimball of Indian kidnapping fame (see the story on the Kimball Farm, page 54) and his brother Timothy. It stands near the site of the Kimball Garrison, and is one of the oldest houses still standing in Hopkinton.

One researcher of the history of this home noted that it was built facing directly west, so that one side faces directly north. This was a common practice at the time and might have been done so the house itself functioned as a sundial!

Like many antique houses in New England, this home started out as a much smaller structure and has been enlarged through the centuries. It grew first from one story to two. In 1820, owner Moses Kimball nearly doubled the size of the place with a new parlor, bedroom and attic.

The use of the house has also varied over the centuries. In the late 1700s, it was a tavern for a while. It probably did a brisk business, as it was situated right on the road from Hopkinton to Concord and Bow.

In the 1930s, it was bought for use as a city dweller's summer residence. Before air conditioning, many Bostonians and New Yorkers would come up here to cool off in the summertime. This home eventually catered to this lively trade as a boarding house.

This picture, created by the current owner of the home, is a view looking from the dining room into the living room in the oldest part of the house. There is a beehive oven behind the cupboard door, and traditional Colonial paneling over the fireplace. The hooks for the old cooking cranes are still in place.

MARY FRENCH

Mary French is a poetry and education advocate, and an avid cook for her large family. The visual arts, literature and good cooking are the celebrations of dear ones past and present. She makes her home in Hopkinton, where she sketches frequently, and paints as often as possible.

Gould Hill Pasta

Serves 4 to 6

2 tablespoons butter

3 tablespoons olive oil

1 large clove garlic, minced

1 onion, diced

2 9-ounce packages frozen artichoke hearts, thawed and drained

2 beef bouillon cubes

1/2 teaspoon dried marjoram

1/4 cup boiling water

1/2 cup chopped parsley

1/4 teaspoon freshly ground pepper

3/4 cup half-and-half

1 pound hot, cooked fettuccini, for serving (spinach pasta works best, and adds color)

freshly grated Parmesan cheese, for serving

In a large saucepan over medium-high heat, melt the butter with the oil. When hot, add the garlic and onion, and sauté until soft. Add the artichokes, and sauté for 2 or 3 minutes longer. Meanwhile, dissolve the bouillon cubes with the marjoram in the boiling water. Add this to the artichoke mixture along with the parsley. Reduce the heat, and let simmer for 5 to 10 minutes, stirring frequently, until the artichokes are just tender. Add the pepper and half-and-half, and let simmer for 5 minutes. Taste for seasoning, and add a little more half-and-half if the sauce is too thick. Serve over hot, cooked fettuccini, with Parmesan cheese.

Smoked Salmon Ravioli

Created by Chef Peter Willis of the 1785 Inn & Restaurant
Serves 8 (3 ravioli per portion)

For the pasta:

2 cups flour

2 eggs plus 2 egg yolks, lightly
    beaten

For the Smoked Salmon Mousse:

1 pound smoked salmon

3 eggs

1 cup heavy cream

1/2 teaspoon coarsely ground pepper

2 tablespoons chopped chives

For the sauce:

1 pound grated Gruyère cheese

1 cup (or more) heavy cream

Prepare the pasta:

Mound the flour on a smooth work surface, and make a well in the center. Pour the eggs into the well, and gradually pull the flour into the eggs until it is all incorporated. Finish kneading by hand, adding more flour if needed for a smooth consistency.

Prepare the mousse:

Combine all the ingredients for the Smoked Salmon Mousse, except 1 egg, in the workbowl of a food processor fitted with the steel blade. Process until smooth. In a small bowl, whisk the remaining egg with 2 tablespoons of cold water; reserve this egg wash. Divide the pasta in half, and roll out each half (or feed it through a pasta roller until thin: #6 setting on a machine). Assemble the ravioli on a smooth, floured surface. Lay out the pasta, and spoon the mousse in 24 equal portions two inches apart on one sheet of pasta. Brush egg wash on the pasta between the mounds of mousse, and cover with the second sheet of pasta. Use your finger to press the pasta sheets firmly together between the mounds of mousse. Cut the ravioli apart, and refrigerate or freeze until you are ready to use.

(Continued)

Smoked Salmon Ravioli (continued)

Bring a large pot of lightly salted water to a boil. Add the ravioli, and cook for about 6 minutes. While the ravioli cook, in each of 8 ovenproof plates combine 1 ounce of cheese and 1/8 cup cream. Heat under the broiler until the cheese melts. Divide the ravioli among the plates and sprinkle 1 ounce cheese over each portion. Place under broiler until the cheese browns lightly, and serve at once.

Macaroni, Ham and Cheese Salad

Serves 4 as a main dish, 6 as a side dish

2 cups cooked elbow macaroni

2 cups diced, cooked ham

2 cups diced sharp Cheddar cheese

1 cup cooked peas

1/2 cup freshly grated Parmesan cheese

1/2 teaspoon freshly ground pepper

3/4 cup sour cream

3/4 cup mayonnaise

1/4 cup lemon juice

1/2 teaspoon salt

1/2 teaspoon crushed red pepper

In a large bowl, combine the macaroni, ham, Cheddar cheese and peas. In a small bowl, stir together the remaining ingredients to combine. Add the dressing to the macaroni mixture, and toss gently. Cover tightly, and refrigerate for several hours or overnight. Toss again before serving.

Karen's Pasta

Serves 4 to 6

1 tablespoon olive oil

1 pound sweet Italian sausage, casings removed, crumbled

1 to 2 tablespoons minced garlic

dash of red pepper flakes

2 28-ounce cans crushed tomatoes

1 teaspoon (or to taste) dried oregano

1 jar (any size) marinated artichoke hearts, drained and chopped

1 can (any size) pitted black olives

1 pound penne, ziti, or similar pasta, for serving

freshly grated Parmesan cheese for serving

In a large saucepan, heat the oil over medium-high heat. When it is hot, add the sausage, and brown it thoroughly. Drain off fat. Add the garlic and red pepper, and sauté briefly. Add the tomatoes and oregano, and stir to combine well. Let simmer for 10 to 15 minutes. Stir in the artichoke hearts and olives, and heat thoroughly.

Meanwhile, cook pasta as desired. Serve with the sauce and Parmesan cheese.

"My sister, Karen Polk of Washington, D.C., started this and we all have added to it along the way. It may be made ahead, and it also freezes well. It is a 'no-fail' recipe; other ingredients may be added (browned onion, for example), and quantities of ingredients may be varied." -*Kathleen A. Belko*

The Inn on Newfound Lake

Enjoy spectacular sunsets & unforgettable meals

Since 1840, this inn has been welcoming travelers to its spectacular lakefront location. Guests are greeted with a full veranda overlooking spectacular sunsets on the fourth largest lake in New Hampshire. Over seven acres of lush New Hampshire countryside and a private beach are available for the enjoyment of the Inn's visitors. Located in the foothills of the White Mountains, the Inn is conveniently located to a wealth of year-round activities, including boating, golfing, ice skating, hiking, and both summer and winter fishing. If you want to relax indoors, the Inn offers a Jacuzzi and weight room, as well as a TV and card room. Thirty-one rooms are available to guests, many with private baths. The full-service restaurant and tavern is renowned for its delicious cuisine. A wood-burning stove and views overlooking the lake create the perfect ambiance for an unforgettable meal. The Inn can also accommodate special dining occasions such as weddings, reunions, anniversaries and birthdays.

The Inn on Newfound Lake
Route 3A
Bridgewater, NH 03222
603.744.9111
800.745.7990
Innkeepers Larry DeLangis and Phelps C. Boyce II

New Hampshire Spring Pasta Toss

Created by Chef John Riccelli of The Inn on Newfound Lake

Serves 4 to 6

1 1/2 cups sundried tomato pieces

2 cups warm water

3 tablespoons butter

2 cups fiddleheads, cleaned and blanched

1 1/2 pounds cooked gemelle or any other tubular pasta

10 cloves garlic, roasted and chopped (about 3 tablespoons)

1 1/4 pounds cooked lobster meat, cut into 1-inch pieces

2 tablespoons freshly grated Pecorino Romano cheese

1 1/2 cups wild baby dandelion greens, washed and coarsely chopped

2 tablespoons extra-virgin olive oil

salt and freshly ground pepper to taste

2 tablespoons sunflower seeds toasted

2 tablespoons minced chives

Soak the sundried tomatoes in the warm water for 10 minutes, or until soft. Drain, and save 1 cup of the tomato water. In a large sauté pan, combine the butter, tomatoes, fiddleheads and the tomato water. Cook until the vegetables are heated through, 1 to 2 minutes. Add the pasta, garlic, lobster and cheese. Toss until heated through, 2 to 3 minutes. Add the dandelion greens, oil, salt and pepper. Stir and toss until greens are wilted. Serve at once in a large bowl, sprinkled with the sunflower seeds and chives.

"During the long winter months I long for the first local flavors of spring."

Zucchini Spaghetti Casserole

Serves 6 as a main dish, 8 as a side dish

2 10-ounce packages dried onion soup mix

8 ounces thin spaghetti, strands broken in half

1/3 cup (5 1/3 tablespoons) butter

1/2 to 1 cup chopped green bell pepper

1/2 to 1 cup chopped red bell pepper

1 cup chopped onions

3 cups peeled, chopped zucchini

6 medium-to-large ripe tomatoes, cored and sliced into narrow wedges

1/4 cup minced parsley

1 teaspoon salt

1/4 teaspoon freshly ground pepper

1 1/4 cups shredded Swiss cheese

1 1/4 cups shredded mozzarella cheese

Bring a large saucepan of water to a boil. Add the soup mix, and stir to dissolve. When the mixture returns to a boil, add the spaghetti, and cook until barely tender, about 7 minutes. Drain and reserve.

In a large sauté pan, melt the butter over medium-high heat. Add the peppers and onions, and cook for 5 to 7 minutes, until tender; add a little water if the mixture seems dry. Add the zucchini, cover, reduce heat to medium-low, and continue cooking for 10 minutes. Preheat oven to 350 degrees. Stir in the tomatoes, parsley, salt and pepper, cover, and cook until hot. Stir in the reserved spaghetti. Transfer the mixture to a 15 x 10-inch casserole. Sprinkle with cheeses, and cover with aluminum foil. Bake for 40 minutes. Let stand 10 minutes before serving.

Spinach-Rice Frittata

Serves 4 to 6

1 teaspoon olive or vegetable oil

1 small onion, chopped

1 to 2 cloves garlic, minced

3 eggs

1 1/2 cups milk

salt, freshly ground pepper,
    dried basil and dried oregano
    to taste

3 cups cooked brown rice

1/4 to 1/2 pound fresh spinach,
    or 1/2 to 1 10-ounce package
    frozen spinach, thawed and
    drained

1/2 cup freshly grated Parmesan
    cheese

2 cups shredded mozzarella cheese

Preheat oven to 350 degrees. Grease a 2-quart baking dish. In a small nonstick pan, warm the oil over medium-high heat. Add the onion and garlic, and sauté for 2 minutes, until softened. Remove from heat, and reserve.

In a medium bowl, lightly beat the eggs. Add the milk and seasonings, and combine well. Add the rice, spinach, Parmesan and onion mixture, and combine well. Transfer to the prepared dish, and sprinkle with the mozzarella cheese. Bake for 1 hour, until heated through and golden on top.

New Hampshire Baked Beans

Serves 8 to 12

2 pounds soldier or red kidney beans (dry)

1 medium onion, chopped

1/2 pound salt pork, scored

1 cup (packed) brown sugar

1/2 cup molasses

1/2 cup maple syrup

3 teaspoons dry mustard

salt and freshly ground pepper to taste

Soak the dry beans overnight in cold water to cover. The next morning, parboil the beans until the skin curls when you blow on them.

Preheat oven to 350 degrees. In a pottery bean pot or crockpot, combine the drained beans, onion, salt pork, brown sugar, molasses, maple syrup, mustard, salt and pepper, and water to cover. Bake all day, adding water as needed.

"Grandmother and Mother's Saturday night supper. Serve with ham or hot dogs, brown bread and tossed salad. Even better reheated the next day!" *-Shirley H. Dunlap*

Eating Tradition

Our family eats beans for supper. Tonight I baked the beans using dry birch and oak, split fine for the big old cookstove that came from Grampa Barker. Just last month he decided he could no longer allow the stove houseroom — having replaced it with a brand new Vermont Castings Resolute and toaster oven. He wanted me to have the Glenwood because he thought I'd appreciate it. I do. Grampa bought it secondhand, just after World War I, off a man in town. He bought it to make life easier for his bride, who had until then cooked on a heating stove. Not that she minded so much. In Ireland, her homeland, she would have been cooking on the hearth, over an open peat fire.

To prepare for tonight's baking of the beans, I stripped away seven decades worth of stove grease; they tell me the grease preserved the cast iron. Beneath the hardened layers was chrome edging and ornament, along with the raised lettering "Modern Glenwood F" on the oven door. Against this lettering, long ago, a child pressed her cheek when the stove was red-hot, to see (my aunt confessed years later) how it would feel. Luckily the family lived near a pond. Grampa rushed her to the cold water, dipped her in to cool the burn. There was no scar.

I baked the beans in the heavy stoneware beanpot Grammie Barker always used. My aunt donated the beanpot last Christmas. I guess she thought I'd appreciate it. I do.

The cover is chipped in four places. But neither the cover nor the pot itself is cracked. My grandmother used that pot, I'm told, most of the 30-odd years of her marriage. She resided in a two-room cabin without electricity or indoor plumbing, a cabin in a New Hampshire town striking in its resemblance — steep hills, open fields, rock-strewn woods — to her birthplace: Lahile Woodford, County Galway. I serve the beans on English china, white with red etchings and webbed age cracks so tiny the surfaces of the dinner plates still feel perfectly smooth. On the bottom of each plate, also in red, are lots of numbers, a globe, a ship: "Catherine Mermet," it says. Must be the name of the pattern or the artist - she's no relation of mine. The English branch of the family is called Ford. "W.H. Grindly and Co., England," it says, "trademark."

At the turn of the century, Great-grammie and Great-grampa Ford drove horse and buggy, 30 miles one way, from home to Concord and back to collect the crate. When the china was new, it was saved for special occasions: birthdays, Thanksgiving, Christmas. *(Continued)*

111

Eating Tradition (continued)

Then, when passed to the next generation and the next, the set didn't seem so special anymore, and was used for every day. Now it's antique, and once again remanded to the cupboard for most of the year — only five cups left, seven dinner plates and six dessert, a bone dish, butter pats, a platter, and tureen. Chipped cups, saucers and so forth are said to be stored in somebody's attic but haven't been seen in years. Still, I know they wouldn't have been thrown away.

Our family eats beans for supper: Beans baked in Grampa Barker's stove, bubbling hot in Grammie Barker's pot, spooned on English china passed down the Ford line, mother to daughter to daughter to me.

To eat beans in this house is to eat tradition. My husband and my daughter seem to agree that tradition is delicious. These are red kidney beans soaked overnight in water and soda, then baked all day with salt pork and sliced onion to just the right texture — neither hard nor mushy — beans dark and sweet with molasses, spiced with catsup and dry mustard, juicy but firm enough to mound on the plate: New England, oven-baked beans.

Baked Beans

Serves a crowd

6 pounds navy pea beans

10 medium onions, chopped

1/2- to 3/4-pound piece salt pork

6 to 8 cloves garlic, minced

2 cups maple syrup
   (not pancake syrup)

2 1/2 cups molasses

2 tablespoons salt

2 tablespoons baking soda
   (causes bubbles, add slowly)

2 tablespoons dry mustard

1 tablespoon ground ginger

3/4 cup white vinegar

The night before, sort and rinse the beans. Put them in a large canning pot, cover generously with cold water, and let soak overnight. In the morning, add the onions, and simmer until the skins on the beans start to break, about 30 minutes. Add the remaining ingredients, stir well, and bring to a full boil. Remove from heat, and cover tightly. Place in a 250-degree oven. Bake for at least 8 hours. Keep covered the whole time, and stir (gently) occasionally. Add water only as needed.

Chicken-Pecan Quiche

Created by Chef Lea Greenwood of the Eastman Inn
Serves 6

2 cups finely chopped, cooked
    chicken

1 cup shredded Monterey Jack cheese

1/4 cup finely chopped scallions

1 tablespoon chopped parsley

1 tablespoon flour

1 unbaked 9-inch pie shell

3 eggs, beaten

1 1/4 cups half-and-half

1/2 teaspoon brown mustard

1/2 cup chopped pecans

Preheat oven to 325 degrees.
In a large bowl, combine the chicken, cheese, scallions, parsley and flour. Distribute the mixture over the bottom of the pie shell. In a medium bowl combine the eggs, half-and-half and mustard. Pour this over the chicken mixture, and top with pecans. Bake for 50 to 60 minutes, until a knife inserted near the center comes out clean.

About Like Splitting Rocks

An old-timer named Bill, a native, enjoys splitting boulders. He's good at it. Uses the hammer and chisel method—wedges, half rounds, feathers. To split a stone with a feather—that's really something. Bill can.

Pound, pound, pound! You pound long enough, hard enough, steady enough in the right place on any rock—granite, quartz, feldspar, what have you—it'll give eventually. That's Bill's attitude. "I may not be able to out-muscle that rock," he says, "or outlast it—but I'm pretty sure I can outsmart it."

When he has an audience for rock-splitting, which he usually does because it's so interesting, he'll pound, pound, pound, and the people gather around—children, grown-ups, and so forth. Just as the rock is about to split, he'll tell them: "Now you're about to see something no one has ever seen before."

The rock splits.

And there it is—something no one has ever seen before: The inside of the rock, all its secrets revealed.

Poultry
& Seafood

Bohanan Farm

Bohanan Farm

In 1907, when the Bohanan family moved into this 1805 farmhouse and began to raise dairy cattle, they probably knew the work it would take to feed and milk a herd of Holsteins. What they probably didn't anticipate was what it would take to "swim" them!

The farm's idyllic setting includes the Contoocook River. There has been a river crossing here since a ferry began in the 1760s, followed by the first public bridge in Hopkinton (1772). Tyler Bridge stands there today. But on a night in mid-March, 1936, no one was crossing the Contoocook: Instead, the Contoocook was crossing the valley.

According to Ashton Bohanan, snow was piled above the ell's windows and two feet of river ice remained when the weather suddenly turned warm. Heavy rain began. At first, the family didn't worry much. They finished off the contents of a hand-cranked ice cream freezer before moving most of the furniture upstairs. What was left behind was inundated by nearly five feet of water. By then, through the intensely black night, they could hear brooks rushing from a half mile away and ice chunks hitting the bridge.

The family loosed the cattle but the animals only splashed though the 33-degree water into the higher main barn. Neighbors came to help and, using a hayfork lift, they hoisted calves and smaller animals onto scaffolds. Saving the larger cattle was trickier. Swimming them out one at a time behind a boat proved impossible: the cow would just turn around and tow the rescuers back to the barn! Eventually the rising water forced the cows to swim, but it took two boats to get each to safety.

When the Hurricane of '38 struck only two years later, the Bohanans moved their herd to high ground well before the waters rose.

CHARLOTTE THIBAULT

As a child, Charlotte Thibault thought that being an artist would be exotic, and romantic, and amazingly fun. Creating art isn't nearly so exotic nor romantic as she once imagined, but she thinks it is still amazingly fun. Nature's beauty lures her over old barbed wire fences into local fields where, as an artist, she bears witness to such everyday glories as tall weeds breaking the surface of late-spring snow.

Wolfe's Tavern Varney Island Chicken Sandwich

Created by Executive Chef Alex Roussakis of the Wolfeboro Inn
Serves 4

For the marinade:

1 cup vegetable oil

1/2 cup fresh lemon juice

1/2 teaspoon dried thyme

1 teaspoon ground cumin

1 tablespoon coriander seeds

1 teaspoon freshly ground pepper

1 teaspoon chopped garlic

4 boneless, skinless halved chicken breasts

For the sandwiches:

4 slices havarti cheese

4 "sub-style" French rolls, split

1/4 cup (4 tablespoons) butter, softened

1/2 cup mango chutney

Prepare the marinade:

In a shallow glass dish, whisk the marinade ingredients to combine thoroughly. Add the chicken, turning to coat it well. Cover tightly, and refrigerate for 2 to 24 hours.

Prepare the sandwiches:

When ready to assemble the sandwiches, preheat an outdoor grill or broiler. Drain the chicken, and grill on both sides until thoroughly cooked, about 4 minutes per side. Place 1 slice of cheese on each chicken piece, and allow to melt. Butter and grill the rolls for 1 minute, until toasted. Spread chutney on the bottom of each roll, and top with the chicken. Cover with the top bun, and serve.

"Many of the inn's recipes are named for the beautiful islands on Lake Winnipesaukee. Varney Island is one of those islands. This sandwich has been a local favorite at the Tavern for many years. The marinade is also great with other chicken and pork recipes."

Chicken Casserole

Serves 6

1 teaspoon chopped onion

1 cup diced celery

3/4 cup low-fat mayonnaise

1 cup sliced mushrooms

1 10-3/4 ounce can condensed
  cream of chicken soup

1 8-ounce can sliced water chestnuts

1 teaspoon salt

2 cups diced, cooked chicken

1 cup cornflakes

1/2 cup sliced almonds

1/4 cup (4 tablespoons) butter,
  melted

Preheat oven to 350 degrees. Grease a 9 x 12-inch baking dish. In a medium mixing bowl, combine onion, celery, mayonnaise, mushrooms, soup, water chestnuts and salt. Distribute the chicken in the prepared dish. Spread the mayonnaise mixture over the chicken. Sprinkle with cornflakes and almonds, and drizzle with butter.

Bake uncovered for 35 minutes, until hot and bubbly.

Chicken with Wild Mushrooms and Artichokes

Compliments of the Mount Washington Hotel
Serves 4

4 8-ounce boneless, skinless chicken breasts

1 cup flour

2 tablespoons olive oil or butter

1 tablespoon minced shallot

1/2 cup diced yellow onion

2 tablespoons brandy or dry white wine

1/2 cup chicken broth

1/2 cup cooked artichoke hearts, quartered

1/2 cup julienned shiitaki mushrooms

1 1/2 cups heavy cream

1 tablespoon Dijon-style mustard

1/4 cup fresh thyme leaves

1/4 cup sliced fresh basil

1/4 cup fresh tarragon leaves

salt and freshly ground pepper to taste

For the garnish:

1/2 cup diced tomato (juice and seeds discarded)

1/4 cup minced chives

Lightly dredge the chicken in flour, making sure to coat each piece evenly; shake off any excess flour. In a large sauté pan, warm the oil over medium-high heat. When it is hot, add the chicken, and lightly brown it on both sides. Add the shallot and onion, reduce the heat, and continue cooking until the chicken is done. Remove the chicken, and keep it warm. Deglaze the pan with brandy. Reduce the liquid by half, add the broth, and reduce by half again. Add the artichokes, mushrooms and cream. Bring to a boil, and reduce to a thick, sauce-like consistency. Stir in the mustard, thyme, basil and tarragon thoroughly. Season with salt and pepper. Divide the sauce among 4 hot serving plates. Top each with a portion of chicken, garnish with tomato and chives, and serve at once.

Chicken in Mustard Sauce

Serves 4

1/4 cup (4 tablespoons) butter

2 shallots or 2 small onions, finely chopped

1 tablespoon minced parsley

2 boneless, skinless chicken breast halves

salt and freshly ground pepper to taste

1/2 teaspoon dried oregano

2 tablespoons flour

1/2 cup light cream

1/2 teaspoon lemon juice

1 tablespoon Dijon-style mustard

1 teaspoon dry mustard

1/2 teaspoon salt

1 cup chicken broth

In a large skillet, melt 2 tablespoons of the butter over medium-high heat. Add 1 shallot, and sauté for 1 to 2 minutes, until soft. Stir in the parsley. Add the chicken, and sauté for about 10 minutes, until nicely browned on both sides and cooked through. Season to taste. Remove the chicken to a shallow baking dish, and keep warm.

Add the remaining butter to the skillet. When it is hot, add the remaining shallot and the oregano, and sauté for 2 minutes. Remove the skillet from the heat, and stir in the flour thoroughly. In a medium bowl, whisk together the cream, lemon juice, mustards, salt and broth. Whisk the mixture into the roux in the skillet, and cook over medium heat, stirring constantly, for 3 minutes. Pour this sauce over the chicken, and broil until the top is nicely glazed. Serve at once.

Chicken Monadnock

Created by Chef Mark Drury of The Inn at East Hill Farm
Serves 8

8 boneless, skinless chicken breasts

2 cups Italian seasoned breadcrumbs

2 eggs

1 cup chicken broth

1/3 cup freshly grated Parmesan cheese

1 teaspoon granulated garlic

1/2 teaspoon freshly ground pepper

1/2 teaspoon herb seasoning

3 large tomatoes

8 slices Provolone cheese

Preheat oven to 375 degrees. Place chicken breasts between two sheets of wax paper or plastic wrap, and pound. Flatten to a uniform thickness of 1/2 inch. Place the chicken on a greased sheet pan. In a large bowl, combine the breadcrumbs, eggs, broth, Parmesan cheese, garlic, pepper and herb seasoning thoroughly. Dice one of the tomatoes into 1/4-inch cubes, and stir into the crumb mixture. Spoon the mixture evenly over each chicken breast, and gently pat to a 1/2-inch thickness. Cut the remaining tomatoes into 1/4-inch-thick slices. Place a slice on top of each chicken breast. Cover with parchment paper, and bake for 20 to 30 minutes. Remove paper, and place one slice of Provolone cheese on top of each chicken breast. Continue baking for ten minutes longer, then serve at once.

The Wolfeboro Inn

A prestigious lakeside destination

The charm and ambiance of a country inn is combined with the style and amenities of a full-service resort at this inn. Built in 1812, this beautifully restored Inn is located in the heart of the village of Wolfeboro, "The Oldest Summer Resort in America." The Inn's private sandy beach is located just a short stroll through the beautifully manicured gardens. All rooms feature private baths, telephones and cable TVs. Enjoy views of the lush flower gardens and Wolfeboro Bay from the Steakhouse, while sampling some of the most tender and flavorful aged beef and delicious seafood in the Lakes Region. Included in each guest's stay is a tour of the Eastern end of Lake Winnipesaukee on board the Inn's very own 65-foot excursion boat, the Winnipesaukee Belle. Cozy rooms and New England hospitality make any getaway at the Inn a truly relaxing and memorable experience.

The Wolfeboro Inn
90 North Main Street
Wolfeboro, NH 03894
603.569.3016
800.451.2389
www.wolfeboroinn.com
Owner Tom Kenney

Wolfeboro Inn Pecan Chicken with Franjelico Sauce

Created by Executive Chef Alex Roussakis of the Wolfeboro Inn
Serves 4

For the sauce:

1/2 cup Franjelico liqueur

1/4 cup (4 tablespoons) butter

1/4 cup flour

1/4 cup (packed) brown sugar

2 cups light cream

2 teaspoons commercially prepared chicken broth base

salt and freshly ground pepper to taste

For the chicken:

2 cups seasoned breadcrumbs

2 cups finely chopped pecans

6 eggs

4 6-ounce boneless, skinless chicken breasts

2 cups flour

4 tablespoons olive oil

Prepare the sauce:

In a medium saucepan, bring the liqueur almost to a boil over high heat. Meanwhile, in a small saucepan, melt the butter over medium-high heat. When it sizzles, whisk in flour and cook for 2 minutes, stirring constantly. Remove from heat. Add the remaining ingredients to the liqueur, and whisk over high heat until scalding. Reduce heat to medium, and begin to whisk in the butter and flour roux a little at a time. Continue whisking until all of the roux is added. Keep warm until ready to serve.

Prepare the chicken:

Preheat oven to 350 degrees. In a small bowl, combine the breadcrumbs and the pecans well, and set aside. In a medium bowl, beat the eggs with 1/2 cup water. Dredge each chicken piece with flour, and then dip it in the egg wash, and then coat it well by rolling in the crumbs. Set the coated chicken pieces aside on wax paper or a plate. In a large, oven-safe sauté pan, warm the oil for 5 minutes over medium-high heat. Add the chicken, and quickly brown both sides, 2 minutes per side. Put the pan in the oven, and cook for 10 minutes, or until cooked through. Sauce the chicken, and serve at once.

Chicken Dijonnaise

Created by Chef Michael Hamm, Sr. of Whitney's Inn
Serves 8

1 cup mayonnaise

1/4 cup Dijon-style mustard

1/2 teaspoon dried dill weed

splash of fresh lemon juice

1/4 cup white wine

2 1/2 pounds boneless, skinless
    chicken breast halves

flour, for dredging

1 pound unseasoned breadcrumbs

1/2 cup vegetable oil

Preheat oven to 350 degrees.
In a medium bowl, whisk together the mayonnaise, mustard, dill, lemon juice and wine; measure out and reserve 1/2 cup of this sauce. Dredge the chicken in the flour, and shake off any excess. Roll each piece of chicken first in the sauce, and then breadcrumbs, until thoroughly coated.

In a large skillet, heat the oil over medium-high heat. When it is hot, add the chicken, 4 pieces at a time, and cook for about 1 minute per side, just until golden brown. Transfer the browned chicken to a baking pan, and bake for about 10 minutes, until the juices run clear.

While the chicken bakes, prepare the serving plates by drizzling each decoratively with some of the reserved sauce. When the chicken is done, set a portion of chicken on each prepared plate, and serve at once.

"I recommend a light Sauvignon Blanc to accompany this meal."

Duck Bombay

Created by Executive Chef Joseph Peterson of the Sunset Hill House
Serves 2

1 tablespoon salt
1 teaspoon cracked black pepper
1/2 teaspoon garlic powder
1/2 teaspoon ground ginger
1 3-pound duckling
2 slices bacon, thinly sliced crosswise
1/4 cup thinly sliced green onions
1/4 cup sliced almonds
1 tablespoon mango chutney
1/4 cup brandy

Preheat oven to 350 degrees. In a small bowl, combine the seasonings thoroughly, and rub the mixture onto the duckling (there will be some seasoning left over). Set the duckling on a rack in a deep roasting pan, and roast for one hour; remove from oven, and let cool. Split the duckling in half lengthwise, and remove the breast and leg joint bones, if desired.

In a small skillet, brown the bacon over medium-high heat. Add the green onions and almonds, and sauté until the almonds are golden. Remove from heat and stir in the chutney. Reserve.

Before serving, brown and warm the duckling under a preheated broiler. Arrange it on a serving platter or plates. If the chutney mixture has cooled, heat it carefully until hot. Off the heat, add the brandy, and flame the sauce. Pour Bombay Sauce over the duckling, and serve at once.

"Our most frequently ordered entrée. A great do-ahead dish that takes just minutes to finish!"

Grilled Breast of Duck with Elderberry Chutney and Sweet Potato Hash

Created by Chef John Riccelli of The Inn on Newfound Lake
Serves 4

For the duck:

4 8-to 10-ounce boneless duck breasts, excess skin trimmed and discarded

salt and freshly ground pepper to taste

1/2 cup New Hampshire maple syrup

1/2 cup Dijon-style mustard

1 tablespoon balsamic vinegar

Sweet-potato Hash (recipe on page 89)

Elderberry Chutney (below)

For the Elderberry Chutney:

1 tablespoon olive oil

1/2 cup diced red onions

1 tablespoon freshly grated ginger

1 1/2 cups fresh, wild elderberries, or diced rhubarb

1/2 cup dried cranberries

1/2 cup rice vinegar

1/2 cup honey

1/4 teaspoon red pepper flakes

Prepare the duck:

Prepare a grill. Start cooking when the coals are grey. Season the duck with salt and pepper. Arrange duck on the hot grill skin side down; cook 6 minutes per side for medium doneness. The duck should be firm to the touch. Meanwhile, combine the maple syrup, mustard and vinegar. Brush both sides of the duck with the maple mixture, and cook an additional 30 seconds per side. Remove the duck to a cutting board, and let it rest for 2 minutes. Slice the duck and arrange each sliced breast over a serving of Sweet Potato Hash. Top with a heaping tablespoon of chutney.

Prepare the chutney:

Warm the oil in a medium skillet over medium heat. When it is hot, add the onions and ginger, and cook for 2 to 3 minutes, until the onions are slightly browned. Add the elderberries, cranberries, vinegar, honey and pepper flakes, and cook for 7 to 10 minutes, until of the desired consistency. Remove from heat, let cool. The chutney can be made a day in advance.

"This is a great late-summer dish when elderberries are at their peak. This recipe also works well with chicken instead of duck."

Breast of Duck with Pears and Grand Marnier

Created by Chef de Cuisine Brian Roberge of the Bretton Arms

Serves 4

2 whole duck breasts (from 6-pound ducks), or 2 Cornish hens, wings discarded

coarse or Kosher salt

cracked black pepper

3 ripe pears, 1 reserved whole, the remaining 2 peeled and cored

1 teaspoon Dijon-style mustard

1 cup Grand Marnier liqueur

1 cup honey

1/2 teaspoon ground ginger

freshly ground pepper to taste

Preheat oven to 350 degrees. Heat a large, oven-safe skillet over medium-high heat. Season the duck with salt and cracked pepper. When the skillet is hot, add the duck breasts, fat side down, and cook until golden brown. Turn the duck over, and cook for 1 minute on the other side, until seared. Put the skillet in the oven, and roast for 15 minutes.

While the duck roasts, combine the 2 cored pears, the mustard, liqueur, honey, ginger, salt and ground pepper in a blender or food processor. Purée. Transfer the purée to a small saucepan over medium-high heat, and let simmer for about 20 minutes.

When the duck has roasted for 15 minutes, carefully drain or skim off as much of the rendered fat as possible. Pour the pear sauce over the duck. Set the remaining whole pear in the skillet with the duck, and continue roasting for 15 to 20 minutes, until the juices run clear, or slice the duck before adding the pear sauce, and roast for only 8 to 15 minutes. Slice the whole, roasted pear for a garnish.

Sea Bass with Chipotle Tartar Sauce

Created by Chef Glenn Gonyea of the Chesterfield Inn

Serves 4

For the fish:

4 8-ounce sea bass fillets

1/2 cup cornmeal

1/4 cup olive oil

For the Chipotle Tartar Sauce:

1 ounce dried chipotle peppers
(smoked jalapeno chiles)

1/2 cup sour cream

1/2 cup mayonnaise

1/4 cup lime juice

1 tablespoon capers

1 tablespoon chopped cornichons

1 tablespoon minced fresh dill

2 tablespoons Champagne vinegar

1 tablespoon minced garlic

1 tablespoon Worcestershire sauce

salt and freshly ground pepper to
taste

For the fish:

Preheat oven to 400 degrees. Dust the seabass with cornmeal. In a 15-inch, oven-safe skillet, warm the olive oil over medium-high heat. Sear the coated seabass in the oil until golden brown on both sides. Place the skillet in the oven to cook for 12 to 15 minutes, until the fish is flaky.

Prepare the sauce:

In a small saucepan, cover the peppers with water. Bring to a boil, then remove from heat, cover, and let sit for 15 minutes. Drain the peppers, reserving the cooking liquid. Remove and discard the stems and seeds. Put the peppers and their cooking liquid in a blender, and purée until smooth. Put 1 teaspoon purée in a medium bowl (reserve the remaining purée for other use). Add the remaining sauce ingredients, and whisk to combine well. Serve the sea bass hot, drizzled with the sauce. Serve over toasted couscous or rice.

Seafood Scampi

Created by Chef Steve Jones of The Inn at East Hill Farm
Serves 8 to 12

1/2 cup (8 tablespoons) butter

1/4 cup olive oil

4 cloves garlic, minced

2 tablespoons minced parsley

juice of 2 lemons

2 cups white wine (Pinot Grigio preferred, but Chardonnay or Sauvignon Blanc will do)

2 pounds sea scallops

1 pound small or medium shrimp, peeled

2 pounds haddock (or other firm, white fish), cut into 2-inch pieces

Hot cooked pasta, for serving

In the top of a large double boiler set over simmering water, combine the butter and oil. When the butter has melted, add the garlic. When the garlic becomes translucent, stir in the parsley, lemon juice and wine. When this liquid is hot, add the seafood (this should be about 20 minutes before serving). The scallops will be firm, but not hard, when done. Serve over the pasta of your choice.

Lobster Casserole

Serves 4 to 6

6 tablespoons unsalted butter

1 large onion, diced

1 large green bell pepper, diced

1 cup sliced mushrooms

1 cup heavy cream

1/2 teaspoon dried thyme

1/2 teaspoon paprika

1/2 teaspoon freshly ground pepper

1 1/4 rolls of Ritz crackers, crushed

1 pound of lobster meat, or a mixture of lobster with scallops and shrimp

1 lemon, for serving

Preheat oven to 350 degrees. In a large skillet, melt 2 tablespoons of the butter over medium-high heat. When it is hot, add the onion, bell pepper and mushrooms, and sauté until the onion is translucent. Season the cream with the thyme, paprika and pepper, and add this to the skillet. Take the skillet off the heat, and add 3/4 of a roll of crushed crackers; stir until about the consistency of un-cooked meatloaf. Stir in the lobster meat. Put the mixture in a 9-inch pie pan. Sprinkle with the remaining crackers and dot with the remaining butter. Bake for 20 minutes. Serve hot, with lemon wedges.

"My grandmother was given this recipe when her favorite cafe in Rhode Island closed. It has become a family favorite, and served up to 45 guests at my parents' 50th anniversary. Clam juice may be substituted for cream for a lower-fat dish." - *Jim Kociuba*

Lila's Clam Pie
Serves 4

4 medium potatoes, peeled and sliced 1/4 inch thick

1 ounce salt pork, diced

2 onions, thinly sliced

1 pound clams

salt and freshly ground pepper to taste

pastry for a 9-inch, double-crust pie

Preheat oven to 425 degrees. Cook potatoes until tender; reserve. In a small skillet, fry out the salt pork. Add the onions, and cook until soft; reserve. Steam the clams just until shells open; shell clams, and reserve the clam meat and juices.

Cover the bottom of a 9 x 13-inch baking dish with a layer of potatoes. Cover the potatoes with some of the clams and juice. Repeat the layers. Distribute the salt pork and onion mixture over all. Season with salt and pepper. Roll out the pastry to fit over the pan. Make slits so steam can escape. Bake for 30 to 40 minutes, until browned.

Where Clams Come From

Someone from inland was surprised to see acres of mud pocked with clam breath that had been covered with sea water a couple hours before.

"Where did all the water go?" he said.

"Tide went out," said the clamdigger. "Dontcha know the tide goes out twice a day."

"I knew the tide went out," the inlander said. "But I didn't know the water went with it."

Meats

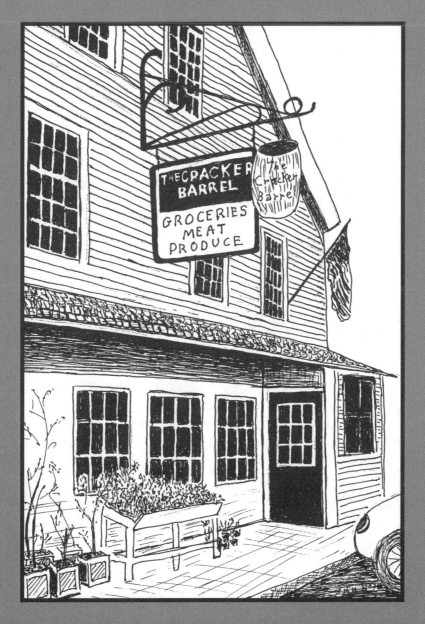

The Cracker Barrel

Cracker Barrel

By 1800, thirteen persons in Hopkinton were being taxed for "stock in trade," which meant that at least some of them were shop proprietors of general stores. Shopping in such an establishment would have been very different from our modern experience. First of all, much of what was displayed on the floor-to-ceiling wooden shelves would have been European-manufactured articles (such as dishes, glassware, shovels, pots and fine woolen cloth), and West Indian products (such as salt, molasses, rum, coffee, rice and sugar).

A good deal of the rest, however, would have been goods produced by fellow shoppers from Hopkinton. For when a woman of that era said she "traded" at a particular store, she meant exactly what she said. She would bring in what she made or raised herself, and use that to trade for what she wanted to buy. According to the researchers at Sturbridge Village, this "country pay" included such products as salt pork, beef pickled in brine, kegs of pickles, firkins of butter and lard, noggins of apple butter, piggins of maple syrup, eggs, chickens, tow cloth, furs and hides. Thus, many early storekeepers seldom received hard cash for their stock. They would take the country pay, assign it a fair value, and enter it as a credit into the long-running — and probably very complicated — account for each household.

This general store in Hopkinton Village was built in 1792. By 1800 it was a store run by Towne and Ballard, storekeepers who "carried on a busy trade and barter." A recent Town Report features a photograph on the cover taken in 1900 from a slightly different angle. Instead of the automobile visible in this drawing, what is parked nearby is a team of oxen and a cart.

MARJORIE NOON

Marjorie Noon studied sculpture at Bennington College, Vermont, and the Art Students League in New York City. Since retiring from teaching art and school administration, she has studied drawing and painting at the University of New Hampshire and, most recently, oil painting at the New Hampshire Institute of Art. She is a juried member of the League of New Hampshire Craftsmen.

Savory Chili

Serves 8 to 10

1 tablespoon vegetable oil

4 stalks celery with leaves, chopped

3 green onions, thinly sliced

5 cloves garlic, chopped

1 large onion, chopped

1 green bell pepper, chopped

2 pounds ground beef

1 15-ounce can tomato sauce

1 6-ounce can tomato paste

1 16-ounce jar salsa

1/2 cup Kahlua liqueur

4 tablespoons chili powder

1 teaspoon salt

dash of pepper

1 16-ounce can kidney beans, undrained

In a 3-quart saucepan, warm the oil over medium-high heat. When it is hot, add the next 5 ingredients and sauté until tender. Add the ground beef, and brown it well, stirring to crumble the meat. Drain well. Meanwhile, put 1 cup water and the remaining ingredients in a slow cooker, and combine well. Add the meat mixture, and stir. Cook on medium heat for 8 to 10 hours.

Can be served with shredded lettuce, shredded cheese, diced onion, tomatoes and tortilla chips.

Gram's Tourtière Pie
Serves 6

1 pound ground pork
1/2 pound ground beef
1 large onion, chopped
1 small clove garlic, minced
1 teaspoon salt
1 teaspoon freshly ground pepper
1 1/4 teaspoons poultry seasoning
1/2 teaspoon celery salt
1/4 teaspoon dried sage
dash of ground cinnamon
2 medium potatoes, peeled, cooked
   and mashed
pastry for a 9-inch, double-crust pie

In a large skillet, combine the pork, beef, onion and garlic over medium-high heat. Cook until the meat is thoroughly browned. Stir in 1/2 cup water, and all the seasonings. Cover, reduce the heat, and let simmer for 20 minutes. Uncover, and continue cooking at a simmer for 5 minutes longer. Remove from heat, and stir in the potatoes.

Preheat oven to 425 degrees. Roll out the pastry, and line a 9-inch pie plate. Fill the pastry with the meat mixture, cover with the remaining pastry, and cut slits to vent. Bake for 15 minutes, then reduce the oven heat to 350 degrees, and continue baking for 25 minutes.

"My mother's family has made this traditional Christmas pie for many generations. It originates from French Canadians, who named it after a pottery casserole dish called a 'tourte.' Families eat 'Tourtière' after Midnight Mass on Christmas Eve." - *Melanie Wheat*

Apple Meat Loaf

Makes 2 loaves, each serving 4 to 6

1 large onion, finely chopped

2 tablespoons butter

2 1/2 pounds ground beef

1 1/2 cups fresh bread cubes

2 cups peeled and finely chopped apples

3 eggs, beaten

1 tablespoon minced parsley

1/2 teaspoon freshly ground pepper

2 tablespoons salt

1/4 teaspoon allspice

1 tablespoon prepared mustard

1/4 cup ketchup

Preheat oven to 350 degrees. Lightly grease two 9 x 5 x 3-inch loaf pans. Sauté onion in butter until soft. In a large mixing bowl, combine all ingredients thoroughly. Divide the mixture between the loaf pans, patting it in firmly. Bake for 1 hour.

Whiting Meat Loaf
Serves 4 to 5

1 pound ground beef
1/3 cup breadcrumbs
1 egg
1/3 cup milk
2 tablespoons chopped onion
1/4 cup ketchup
1/2 teaspoon salt
1/4 teaspoon freshly ground pepper
1/4 teaspoon dried sage
2 tablespoons chopped green bell
    pepper (optional)

For the sauce:
1 1/2 tablespoons brown sugar
1/4 teaspoon grated nutmeg
1/2 teaspoon dry mustard
1/4 cup ketchup

Preheat oven to 350 degrees. In a large bowl, combine the ingredients for the meatloaf thoroughly. Shape the mixture into a loaf in a baking dish, or a 9 x 5-inch pan. In a small bowl, stir together the ingredients for the sauce. Make a slight indentation down the top of the meatloaf, using a spoon. Spread the sauce on the top. Bake for 1 hour.

"This recipe came from my Grandmother Whiting, and has been a family favorite for three generations." *-Beth Bloomquist*

Cumin and Molasses Charred Beef Tenderloin

Created by Executive Chef Jeffrey Woolley of The Manor On Golden Pond
Serves 4 (4 ounces each)

3/4 cup dark molasses

1/4 cup balsamic vinegar

1/2 cup red wine

2 tablespoons ground cumin

salt and freshly ground pepper to taste

1 pound beef tenderloin, trimmed of fat

In a glass or other non-reactive dish just large enough to hold the beef, combine the molasses, vinegar, wine and seasonings. Put the beef in the marinade, and turn to coat; cover tightly and refrigerate. Let the beef marinate overnight, turning occasionally.

When ready to cook, preheat the oven to 350 degrees. Remove the beef from the marinade. In a large, cast-iron skillet heated until very hot, sear all sides of the beef until black and charred. Carefully transfer the skillet to the oven, and roast to desired doneness, about 30 to 40 minutes for medium. Slice, and serve with mashed potatoes and gravy.

Beef Tenderloin with Herb-roasted Vegetables

Serves 4 to 6

2 tablespoons butter

2 tablespoons olive oil

12 small red, new potatoes

8 tiny white onions, skinned, ends trimmed

3 large carrots, peeled and cut into chunks

8 whole garlic cloves, peeled, plus 3 cloves garlic, coarsely chopped

8 sprigs fresh thyme or 1 teaspoon dried thyme

12 medium mushrooms

1 teaspoon salt

2 tablespoons grainy, Dijon-style mustard

1 teaspoon coarse black pepper

1/2 beef tenderloin (about 3 pounds) trimmed of fat and tied

2 zucchini, cut into quarters lengthwise, then halved

Preheat oven to 500 degrees. In a large, nonstick skillet, heat 1 tablespoon of the butter and 1 tablespoon of the oil over medium-high heat. When it is hot, add the potatoes, onions, carrots, whole garlic cloves, and half of the thyme, and lower the heat to medium. Sauté for 8 to 10 minutes. Add the mushrooms and sauté 5 minutes longer. Sprinkle the vegetables with salt, reduce the heat to low, and cook, covered 12 to 15 minutes. Meanwhile, in a small bowl, combine the mustard, pepper and the chopped garlic. Spread this mixture evenly over the beef with your fingers. Place the beef in a roasting pan. Arrange the vegetables from the skillet, and the zucchini, around the roast. Drizzle the remaining 1 tablespoon oil over the vegetables, dot with the remaining 1 tablespoon butter, and season with the rest of the thyme. Place the pan in the oven, and reduce the heat to 375. Bake for 25 to 30 minutes for rare (120 degrees F on a meat thermometer), or 35 to 40 minutes for medium (140 degrees F). Baste the meat and stir the vegetables several times during roasting. Remove the pan from the oven, and let stand for 10 minutes before slicing. Place the beef on a platter, remove the string, and surround it with vegetables.

Pork Chops Supreme

For each serving:
1 1-inch-thick pork chop
salt
1 thin slice lemon
1 thick slice onion
2 teaspoons brown sugar
1 to 2 tablespoons catsup

Preheat oven to 350 degrees. Put the desired number of chops in a baking dish. Season with salt, and cover with the lemon and onion. Sprinkle with brown sugar, then spread with catsup to cover. Cover and bake for 1 hour. Uncover, and continue baking for 30 minutes, basting occasionally.

A Hankering for Venison

"Yup, Ma was the only one who bagged a deer this season."
 "What did she use?"
"Chevy Nova."

Loin of Pork with Port Sauce

Created by Dennis and Roberta Aufranc at Maple Hill Farm

Serves 4

olive oil, for sautéing

2-pound loin of pork, sliced into 8 equal portions

1 tablespoon fresh sage, minced

salt and freshly ground pepper to taste

1 cup Port wine

Cover the bottom of a large sauté pan with a film of oil. Dip the pork in the oil, and season both sides with sage, salt and pepper. Over medium-high heat, warm the oiled pan. When it is hot, gently add the meat, and sauté until nicely colored (caramel); turn, and let the second side color nicely, cooking until done, about 4 to 5 minutes per side. Remove the meat to a warm plate, and keep warm. Add the Port to the pan, scraping up any browned bits, and reduce the Port until it is the thickness of cream. Pour the sauce over the meat, and serve with Browned Potatoes (page 93).

Orange-Glazed Pork Loin

Created by Chef Tracy Foor of the Mountain Lake Inn
Serves 12 to 16

1 clove garlic, minced
1 teaspoon salt
1/4 teaspoon dried thyme
1/4 teaspoon ground ginger
1/4 teaspoon freshly ground pepper
1 rolled boneless pork loin roast,
   about 8 pounds

For the glaze:
1/4 cup (packed) brown sugar
1 tablespoon cornstarch
1 cup orange juice
1 tablespoon Dijon-style mustard

Preheat oven to 350 degrees.
In a small bowl, or mortar and pestle, mash together the garlic, salt, thyme, ginger and pepper. Rub this mixture over the pork. Place the pork, fat side up, on a rack in a roasting pan. Roast, uncovered, for 2 hours.

Prepare the glaze:
In a small saucepan, thoroughly combine the brown sugar and cornstarch. Add the remaining ingredients and 1/3 cup water, and whisk until smooth. Bring to a boil, and boil for 2 minutes, stirring constantly. Brush the glaze over the pork, and continue roasting 1 hour longer (total roasting time is 3 hours), brushing occasionally with glaze. Let the pork stand 10 minutes before slicing.

"This is one of the best recipes I've ever tried. Guests always want the recipe. The rub and glaze are also great on pork chops."

The Mount Washington Hotel & Resort

A legendary "Grand Dame" in the heart of the White Mountains

Since 1902, The Mount Washington Hotel & Resort has offered visitors a tradition of gracious leisure, timeless elegance and world-class cuisine. This National Historic Landmark has been a favorite summer haunt for poets, presidents and princes through the years. Guests can enjoy golf, tennis, horse-back riding, carriage rides, hiking, children's programs, swimming, and both alpine and Nordic skiing. Come inside and enjoy the services in the health spa, relax in a Jacuzzi or by the fireplace. After a full day of activity, slip into the evening hours with a gourmet dinner and live entertainment. Choose to dine in any of the seven restaurants, which offer everything from elegant, four-course dinners to casual pub fare. After dinner, unwind with a moonlight stroll on the veranda, listen to jazz music in the snug lounge, or dance one more waltz as the orchestra plays on. There is something for everyone at this Resort.

The Mount Washington Hotel & Resort
Route 302
Bretton Woods, NH 03575
603.278.1000
800.258.0330 www.mtwashington.com

Glazed Pork Tenderloin with Braised Red Cabbage

Compliments of the Mt. Washington Hotel & Resort

Serves 6

For the pork:

2 1/2-pound pork tenderloin

salt and freshly ground black pepper to taste

1/2 cup honey

1/2 cup whole-grain mustard

1 1/2 cups almonds, finely chopped by hand or coarsely ground in a food processor

2 tablespoons olive oil

For the cabbage:

4 cups sliced red cabbage (one small head)

1/2 cup brandy

2 tablespoons (packed) brown sugar

1/4 cup balsamic vinegar

1 pinch allspice

1 pinch coriander

1 cup peeled, diced apple

1 cup fresh cranberries, chopped (or 1/2 cup dried cranberries)

2 tablespoons butter (optional)

salt

freshly ground black pepper

For the garnish:

1 whole apple, thinly sliced

Prepare the pork:

Preheat oven to 375 degrees. Remove and discard fat from pork. Rinse pork under cold water, and pat dry with paper towel. Season with salt and pepper. In a small bowl, combine honey and mustard. Coat pork with all the mustard mixture, then roll in almonds, using your hands to press the nuts onto the meat, to coat thoroughly.

In a large sauté pan, warm the olive oil over medium-high heat until hot. Add the pork, and sauté for 10 minutes, until golden brown. Transfer the pork to an ungreased baking sheet. Bake for 30 minutes, or until an instant-reading meat thermometer registers 170 degrees. Remove from oven, and let stand for 10 minutes.

Prepare the cabbage:

Meanwhile, in a large pot, combine the cabbage, brandy, brown sugar and vinegar over medium heat. Sauté briefly. Add allspice, coriander, apple and cranberries, and let simmer for 8 minutes. Remove from heat, and add butter, salt and pepper. Divide the cabbage among 6 dinner plates. Cut the pork into 1-inch-thick slices. Arrange the pork over each serving of cabbage, garnish and serve.

1812 Steakhouse Rack of Lamb with Sweet, Garlic Demi-Glace

Created by Chef Aaron Morrissey of the Wolfeboro Inn
Serves 4

For the sauce:

2 cups demi-glace, prepared from a commercial mix

1 tablespoon chopped garlic

1/2 cup honey

freshly ground pepper to taste

For the lamb:

2 cups seasoned breadcrumbs

1 teaspoon chopped fresh rosemary

2 tablespoons olive oil

2 20-ounce Frenched racks of lamb (cut in half, to fit into the sauté pan)

1 cup Dijon-style mustard

For the garnish:

cherry tomatoes and fresh rosemary sprigs

Prepare the sauce:

Make the demi-glace as directed. When it is thick, keep it over medium heat, add the remaining ingredients, and let simmer for 5 minutes. Keep warm until ready to serve. The sauce may be prepared 2 days in advance, tightly covered and refrigerated.

Prepare the lamb:

Preheat oven to 350 degrees. In a small bowl, combine the breadcrumbs and rosemary well, and set aside. In a medium, oven-safe sauté pan, warm the oil for 2 minutes over medium-high heat. Add the lamb and quickly brown both sides, about 3 minutes per side. Brush the entire lamb with mustard, and then roll it in the crumbs to coat thoroughly. Return the coated lamb to the pan, put the pan in the oven, and cook for 10 to 15 minutes (10 for rare, and 15 for medium to well). Remove from oven and let rest for 10 minutes. To serve, slice the lamb on every bone or every other bone, fan out the pieces on serving plates, sauce with the warm demi-glace, and garnish with a skewered cherry tomato, and fresh rosemary sprigs.

Pies & Cakes

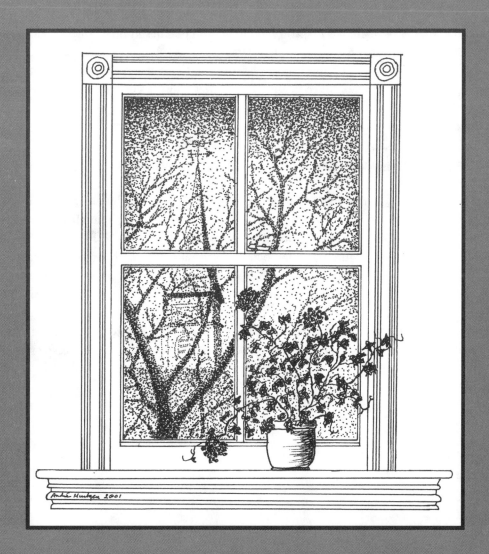

Church Spire

Church's Spire

During the 1800s, there were a growing number of churches in the villages of Hopkinton. These churches were credited with improving the image of the town. For example (according to the booklet published to celebrate the 125th anniversary of the United Methodist Church in Contoocook Village), the Methodist circuit riders were "a power for good, especially on the frontier areas of the western and northern portions of the state." Furthermore, those drawn to Methodism at the time were generally "on the side of liberal and reform thinking." By the middle of the century, the number of Methodists in New Hampshire was second only to the number of Congregationalists.

As early as 1842, there were Methodists in Hopkinton, as shown by the fact they received part (albeit small) of the "minister tax" collected by the town. For a number of years, they gathered at Hopkinton Academy, and then at a shop in Contoocook. Finally, in 1871, the Methodists erected a church in Contoocook Village at a cost of about two thousand dollars. In *Life and Times in Hopkinton, New Hampshire*, C.C. Lord calls this church building "a neat and tasty edifice." That church's spire is visible through the window of this drawing.

Centenarian Dorothy Osborne recalls that there was always a barrel at the United Methodist Church for members to fill with cast-off clothes to be sent to missionaries.

ANDRÉ HURTGEN

For André Hurtgen, making art is perhaps the most enjoyable way to relax. As language teacher at St. Paul's School in Concord, he found great satisfaction in painting as a way to escape the round-the-clock pressures of boarding school life. He added brushes to his lifelong skill of drawing. He likes to work in watercolors mostly, and pen and ink occasionally. A year's study of calligraphy while living in Tokyo defined for him the extraordinary importance of detail, which can be appreciated in the "dot" technique used here.

Fluffy Peanut Butter Pie

Serves 6

8 ounces cream cheese, softened
1/2 cup peanut butter
1 cup confectioners' sugar
1/2 cup milk
8 ounces whipped topping
1 9-inch chocolate crumb pie shell
1/4 cup finely chopped pecans
1/4 cup chocolate syrup

In a large mixing bowl, beat the cream cheese until light and fluffy. Add the peanut butter and sugar, and beat well. Gradually add the milk, and continue beating until smooth. Fold in the whipped topping. Spoon this mixture into the pie shell, smooth the top, and sprinkle with pecans. Freeze until firm. Drizzle with chocolate syrup before serving.

Adapted from "A Slice of Paradise" cookbook of the Naples Community Hospital Auxiliary, Naples, Florida. - *Sara McNeil*

Coffee Buttercrunch Pie

Created by Becky Mallar of The 1785 Inn & Restaurant
Serves 8

For the crust:

1/2 package pie crust mix

1 ounce unsweetened chocolate, grated (a food processor makes this easy)

1/4 cup (packed) light brown sugar

1 cup finely chopped walnuts

1 teaspoon vanilla extract

For the filling:

1/2 cup (8 tablespoons) butter, softened

1 scant cup (packed) light brown sugar

1 ounce unsweetened chocolate, melted and cooled

2 1/2 teaspoons instant coffee

2 eggs

For the topping:

1 pint (16 ounces) heavy cream

1 tablespoon instant coffee, ground to a powder

1/2 cup confectioner's sugar

Prepare the crust:

Preheat oven to 375 degrees. Line a 9-inch pie plate with aluminum foil. In a large mixing bowl, stir together the pie crust mix, chocolate, sugar and nuts. Combine the vanilla and 1 tablespoon water, and drizzle this all over the crust mixture while stirring (do not pour it into one spot). The consistency should be lumpy and crumbly; it will hold together in the pan. Press the mixture all around the sides and bottom of the prepared pie plate. Bake for 15 minutes. Let cool.

Prepare the filling:

In a small mixing bowl, cream the butter. Gradually add the sugar, and beat at high speed for 2 to 3 minutes. Beat in the chocolate and instant coffee. Add the eggs, one at a time, stirring them in with a rubber spatula.

Pour the filling into the cooled crust and place in the freezer until frozen. This should take a couple of hours. Carefully lift the foil out of the plate. Using a knife warmed in hot water (wipe off excess water each time you dip the knife in the water), cut the pie into 8 pieces.

(continued)

Coffee Buttercrunch Pie (continued)

Prepare the topping:

In a chilled medium bowl, whip together the topping ingredients until stiff. Divide the topping among the 8 portions of pie, and serve at once. This recipe can be doubled, and frozen.

Pineapple Pie

Serves 6 to 8

2 eggs
1 cup sugar
2 tablespoons flour
1 pinch salt
1 20-ounce can crushed pineapple
   in its own juice
pastry for 9-inch double-crust pie

Preheat oven to 425 degrees. In a medium bowl, beat the eggs until light. Beat in the sugar, flour and salt. Add pineapple, and stir to mix well. Place one pastry crust into a 9-inch pie plate, and pour in the pineapple mixture. Cover with top crust, seal the edge of the crust and cut slits in the top of the crust to vent. Bake for 35 minutes, until the bottom crust is thoroughly cooked.

Grandma's Apple Pie
9-inch pie

For the pastry:
1 cup vegetable shortening
2 cups flour
1/3 cup milk
1 tablespoon vinegar

For the filling:
7 to 8 cups sliced, peeled tart apples
3/4 cup sugar
2 tablespoons flour
1/4 teaspoon salt
1/4 teaspoon grated nutmeg
1/4 teaspoon ground cinnamon
2 tablespoons butter

Prepare the pastry:

In a medium bowl, cut the shortening into the flour until crumbly. Add the milk and vinegar gradually, tossing with a fork until all the flour is moistened, and the pastry comes away from the side of the bowl. Gather it into a ball, wrap in plastic, and chill about 20 minutes.

Preheat oven to 400 degrees.

Prepare the filling:

In a large bowl, toss the apples, sugar, flour, salt and spices together. Divide the pastry in half, and roll each piece to fit a 9-inch pie pan. Line the pie pan with pastry, and add the apples. Dot the apples with butter. Cover with the second round of pastry, and cut vents in the top crust. Bake for about 1 hour, until light golden-brown, and the juices bubble.

"My grandmother used to make this pie for holidays." *-Tammy Clay*

Chocolate Fudge Cake
Serves 12

1/4 cup vegetable shortening
2 ounces unsweetened chocolate
1 cup sugar
1 cup flour
1/2 teaspoon salt
1/2 teaspoon baking powder
1 egg
1/2 teaspoon baking soda
1/4 cup sour cream
1 teaspoon vanilla extract

Preheat oven to 350 degrees. Grease a 8 x 8-inch baking pan. In the top of a double boiler set over simmering water, melt the shortening and chocolate. Remove from heat, and stir in the sugar and 1/2 cup water. Let cool.

In a small bowl, combine the flour, salt and baking powder. Add the egg to the cooled chocolate mixture, and combine well. Stir in the flour mixture thoroughly. Dissolve the baking soda in the sour cream, and add this to the batter along with the vanilla. Combine thoroughly. Pour the batter into the prepared pan, and bake for 35 minutes, until tester comes out clean.

German Chocolate Cake Frosting
Makes enough to frost a 2-layer, 8-inch cake

1 cup evaporated milk
1 cup sugar
3 egg yolks
1/2 cup margarine
1 teaspoon vanilla extract
1 1/3 cups sweetened, flaked coconut
1 cup pecans, chopped

In a 1-quart saucepan, combine the first five ingredients and cook over medium heat until thick, about 12 minutes. Remove from heat, add the coconut and pecans, and stir to combine thoroughly.

Cabernet Inn

A vintage bed & breakfast

Award-winning perennial gardens, scrumptious breakfasts and engaging hosts make this romantic and elegant 1842 inn unforgettable. The Inn is set among towering pines just a stroll away from breathtaking views of Mt. Washington. Eleven exquisitely maintained guest rooms feature queen beds, private baths, gas fireplaces and Jacuzzi tubs for two. Cozy up to the fire in the quiet upstairs living room with your favorite book, or relax in the comfy downstairs gathering room and watch TV or a movie. Innkeepers Rich and Debbie Howard will start your day with a bountiful country breakfast, including farm-fresh eggs, old-fashioned pancakes, omelets made to order, and sizzling bacon or sausage. Enjoy your breakfast in the dining room or al fresco on the deck surrounded by the beauty of nature at its finest. The Inn is minutes to all outdoor activities, including skiing, golf, hiking, mountain biking and outlet shopping. Cabernet Inn is completely smoke-free and handicapped accessible.

Unforgettably romantic, exquisitely maintained, simply elegant.

Cabernet Inn
PO Box 489
North Conway, NH 03860
603.356.4704
800.866.4704
www.cabernetinn.com
Innkeepers Rich and Debbie Howard

Never-fail Sponge Cake

Created by Chef Debbie Howard of the Cabernet Inn
Serves 12 to 14

4 eggs, separated
1 cup sugar
1/4 cup cold water
1 cup sifted cake flour
1 teaspoon baking powder

Preheat oven to 325 degrees. In a large mixing bowl, combine the egg yolks and sugar, and beat until very light. Beat in the cold water. Sift together the flour and baking powder, and add to the egg-yolk mixture; beat to combine well. Beat the egg whites until stiff. Fold them into the batter, and scrape the resulting mixture into a well-greased 8-cup angel food pan.

Bake for about 30 minutes, until the top is golden brown. Remove from oven, and let cool completely before unmolding.

"This makes a wonderful light summer dessert, and is always the most requested cake for our family birthdays. To serve, slice the cake in half horizontally, and fill with whipped cream. Top with additional whipped cream and strawberries."

English Toffee Heaven

Created by Chef Mimi Atwood of The Benjamin Prescott Inn
Serves 10 to 12

1 18-ounce package butter-flavored cake mix

2/3 cup vegetable oil

4 eggs

8 ounces sour cream

1 cup (loosely packed) brown sugar

1/3 cup finely chopped pecans (optional)

2 teaspoons ground cinnamon

1/2 cup Skor's English Toffee Bits

1/4 cup confectioners' sugar

1/4 cup half-and-half or cream

Preheat oven to 325 degrees. Grease or spray a 13 x 9 x 2-inch glass baking pan. In a large mixing bowl, beat together the cake mix, oil, eggs and sour cream on medium speed for 2 minutes, scraping the bowl occasionally. Spread half of the batter in the prepared pan. In a medium bowl, combine the brown sugar, pecans, cinnamon and toffee bits, and sprinkle this mixture evenly over the batter. Carefully spread the remaining batter over the filling.

Bake for about 35 minutes, until golden brown and a toothpick inserted in the center comes out clean. Remove from oven and prick the surface of the warm cake several times with a fork. Stir together the confectioners' sugar and half-and-half to make a smooth glaze. Brush glaze over the cake, using a pastry brush. Let cool completely so the layers hold together.

"Reheat in a 300 degree oven for about twenty minutes if you wish to serve this warm. Enjoy, and don't ever tell anybody how easy it is."

Choco Dot Pumpkin Cake
Serves 12 to 15

2 cups sifted flour

2 teaspoons baking powder

1 teaspoon baking soda

1/2 teaspoon salt

1 1/2 teaspoons ground cinnamon

1/2 teaspoon ground cloves

1/4 teaspoon allspice

1/4 teaspoon ground ginger

2 cups sugar

4 eggs

2 cups fresh pumpkin (or 1 15-ounce can)

1 cup vegetable oil

1 1/2 cups 100% bran flakes

1 6-ounce package (1 cup) chocolate chips

1 cup coarsely chopped nuts

Preheat oven to 350 degrees. In a medium bowl, sift together the flour, baking powder, baking soda, salt, spices and sugar. Set aside. In a large mixing bowl, beat the eggs until foamy. Add the pumpkin, oil and bran flakes; mix well. Add the sifted dry ingredients, and mix only until combined. Stir in the chips and nuts. Scrape the batter into an ungreased 4-inch tube pan, and smooth the top. Bake for about 1 hour and 10 minutes, until a toothpick inserted near the center comes out clean. Let cool completely before removing from pan. Place on cake plate; drizzle with confectioner's sugar glaze, if desired.

"My grandmother, who was born in 1877, used to make this every Thanksgiving with fresh pumpkin. I looked forward to having this every year, and still make it quite often. Delicious with or without glaze." - *Ida Mae T. Rondeau*

Chocolate Strawberry Shortcake

Created by Chef Becky Mallar of The 1785 Inn & Restaurant
Serves 12 to 15

For the biscuits:

2 cups flour

2 teaspoons baking powder

4 tablespoons unsweetened cocoa

1/3 cup granulated sugar

1 teaspoon baking soda

1/2 teaspoon salt

5 tablespoons cold, unsalted butter, cut into five portions

4 ounces (2/3 cup) chocolate chips

3/4 cup milk

For the sauce:

4 quarts strawberries, hulled

2 cups granulated sugar

1/2 cup orange juice

For the whipped cream:

2 cups heavy cream

1/2 cup confectioners' sugar

1 teaspoon vanilla extract

Prepare the biscuits:

Preheat oven to 350 degrees. In the workbowl of a food processor fitted with the steel blade, combine the flour, baking powder, cocoa, sugar, baking soda and salt, and process well. Add the butter and chocolate chips, and process until crumbly. With the machine running, add the milk and process until the mixture is crumbly but holds together when pinched. Turn the dough out onto a clean work surface, shape it into a ball, then flatten it into a circle approximately 1 inch thick.

Using a 2-inch round cutter, cut out 12 to 15 shortcakes. Place them on a cookie sheet lined with parchment paper. Bake for 10 to 12 minutes. When slightly cooled, cover them with plastic wrap to keep them moist.

Prepare the sauce:

Purée 2 quarts of the strawberries in a food processor. Slice the remaining berries. In a large bowl, combine the purée, the sugar and orange juice. Stir the sliced berries into the puréed mixture.

(continued)

Chocolate Strawberry Shortcake (continued)

Prepare the whipped cream:

In a chilled, large mixing bowl, whip the cream on high speed. When the mixture begins to thicken, beat in the sugar and vanilla.

Assemble the shortcakes:

Place a tablespoon of sauce in the bottom of each serving dish. Split the biscuits in half. Place the bottom half of a biscuit on the sauce. Top with 2 tablespoons sauce, and 1 tablespoon whipped cream. Add the top half of the biscuit, 2 more tablespoons sauce and finally 1 tablespoon whipped cream. Garnish with fresh mint leaves if desired.

Harvest Cake

Serves 12

For the cake:

4 cups chopped, peeled apples
   (4 to 6 apples)

2 cups sugar

3 cups flour

2 teaspoons baking soda

1 teaspoon salt

1 teaspoon vanilla extract

1 cup vegetable shortening

1 cup walnuts (optional)

2 eggs, well beaten

For the glaze:

1/2 cup (8 tablespoons) butter

1 cup brown sugar (packed)

1/4 cup milk

Butter and flour a 9 1/2-inch tube pan. In a medium bowl, toss the apples with the sugar. Let stand for 1 hour.

Preheat oven to 350 degreese. In a large mixing bowl, thoroughly combine the remaining ingredients for the cake. Add the apple mixture, and stir well. Scrape the batter into the prepared pan. Bake for 50 to 60 minutes, until tester comes out clean. Let cool slightly. Turn out onto serving dish.

When the cake is nearly done, prepare the glaze: Combine the ingredients in a small saucepan over medium-high heat. Stirring constantly, bring to a boil. Let boil for 2 1/2 minutes. Pour glaze over the warm cake.

Dutch Apple Cake
Serves 4

For the cake:

1 1/4 cups flour

1 tablespoon baking powder

1/4 teaspoon salt

1 teaspoon sugar

1/2 cup (8 tablespoons) butter, softened

1 egg yolk

2 tablespoons milk

3 cups peeled, sliced MacIntosh apples

For the topping:

3/4 cup sugar

1 1/2 tablespoons flour

1/4 teaspoon ground cinnamon

2 tablespoons butter

Prepare the cake:

Preheat oven to 350 degrees. In a medium bowl, sift together the flour, baking powder, salt and sugar.

Cut in the butter, as for pie crust, until pieces are the size of peas. In a small bowl, stir together the egg yolk and milk, and add this mixture to the flour mixture. Using your hand, work the mixture into a soft dough.

Press the dough into a 7 x 11-inch baking pan. Distribute the apples evenly over the dough.

Prepare the topping:

In a small bowl, combine the topping ingredients, and cut or rub the butter in to make a crumbly consistency. Sprinkle this over the apples. Bake for about 50 minutes, until tester comes out clean.

Rhubarb Cake

Created by Chef Joan DeBrine of Maple Hedge Bed & Breakfast
Serves 6 to 8

For the cake:
1 cup sugar
1 egg
2 cups flour
1/2 teaspoon baking powder
1 cup buttermilk
2 tablespoons butter, melted
1 1/3 to 2 cups diced rhubarb

For the topping:
2 tablespoons butter, melted
1/2 cup sugar

For the sauce:
1/2 cup sugar
1/2 cup (8 tablespoons) butter
1/2 cup evaporated milk
2 teaspoons vanilla extract

Preheat oven to 350 degrees. Grease a 9-inch square pan.

Prepare the cake:
   In a medium mixing bowl, beat the sugar and egg until smooth. Stir together the dry ingredients, and add to the egg mixture. Stir in the buttermilk mixed with butter. Mix well. Stir in the rhubarb. Spread evenly in the prepared pan.

Prepare the topping:
   In a small bowl, stir together the butter and sugar well; spread this over the cake batter. Bake for 45 minutes, until a toothpick inserted near the center comes out clean.

Prepare the sauce:
   In a medium saucepan, combine the sugar, butter and evaporated milk over medium-high heat. Bring to a boil, stirring constantly. Let boil for 1 minute. Remove from heat, and stir in the vanilla. Serve hot over the cake.

"This recipe won 1st place for desserts in a local newspaper contest. It is as good, or better, on the second day."

Cranberry Cake
Serves 8 to 10

For the cake:
3 tablespoons butter, melted
1/2 cup sugar
2 cups flour
3 teaspoons baking powder
pinch of salt
1 cup milk
2 cups fresh cranberries

For the sauce:
1 cup sugar
1/2 cup (8 tablespoons) butter
3/4 cup heavy cream

Preheat oven to 350 degrees. Butter a 10 x 6-inch Pyrex baking dish.

Prepare the cake:
In a medium bowl, combine the butter and sugar thoroughly. In a separate bowl, sift together the flour, baking powder and salt. Add the flour mixture to the butter mixture alternately with the milk, stirring thoroughly after each addition. Fold in the cranberries. Scrape the batter into the prepared baking dish, and bake for about 45 minutes, until a toothpick inserted near the center comes out clean.

When the cake is nearly done, prepare the sauce.

Prepare the sauce:
In a medium saucepan, combine the sugar, butter and cream over medium-high heat. Bring just to a boil, then serve hot with the warm cake.

"From the 40 Leaguers' 1956 cookbook. My mother was a member of this service club. This is a really yummy cake — nice for the holidays. This cake should be served warm." - *Diane Myler*

Pineapple Upside-down Cake
Serves 12 to 16

1/3 cup (5 1/3 tablespoons) butter

1/2 cup (packed) brown sugar

1 20-ounce can pineapple rings or
    sliced pineapple

1 10-ounce can maraschino cherries

1 1/3 cups flour

1 cup sugar

2 teaspoons baking powder

1/2 teaspoon salt

1/3 cup vegetable shortening

2/3 cup milk

1 teaspoon vanilla extract

1/2 teaspoon lemon extract

1 egg

whipped cream, for serving

Preheat oven to 350 degrees. Put the butter in a 9-inch square baking dish or 10-inch oven-proof skillet, and set in the oven until the butter melts. Sprinkle the brown sugar evenly over the melted butter, and arrange the pineapple and cherries in the sugar mixture.

In a medium mixing bowl, combine the flour, sugar, baking powder and salt. Add the shortening, milk, vanilla and lemon extract, and beat for 2 minutes. Add the egg, and beat for 1 minute longer. Pour the batter over the fruit. Bake for 40 to 50 minutes, until golden brown. Serve with whipped cream.

Apricot-brandy Pound Cake

Created by Chef Lea Greenwood of the Eastman Inn
Serves 15 to 20

1 cup (16 tablespoons) butter, softened

3 cups sugar

6 eggs

3 cups flour

1/2 teaspoon salt

1/4 teaspoon baking soda

1 cup sour cream

1 teaspoon orange extract

1 teaspoon vanilla extract

1/2 teaspoon lemon extract

1/2 teaspoon rum extract

1/4 teaspoon almond extract

1/2 cup apricot brandy

confectioners' sugar, for dusting

Preheat oven to 325 degrees. Grease and flour a 10-inch tube pan. In a large mixing bowl, cream the butter and sugar. Add the eggs one at a time, beating well after each addition. In another bowl, whisk together the flour, salt, and baking soda. In a third bowl, combine the sour cream, flavorings, and brandy. Alternately add the flour and sour cream to the butter mixture, beginning and ending with flour. Beat well. Pour the batter into the prepared pan. Bake for 80 to 90 minutes, until the cake pulls slightly from the sides of the pan. Let the cake cool in the pan for 30 minutes. Carefully invert the pan on a rack to remove the cake, turn the cake right side up, and allow to cool completely before slicing. Dust the cooled cake with confectioners' sugar.

"This cake is marvelous the first day, but even better on the second or third day!"

165

The Well

Urban: There's all kinds of stuff in the ground around my place. Mica, feldspar, quartz, beryl. You better go careful when you're digging. Don't know what you're going to find. Nineteen sixty-two, Mother got it into her head she wanted a well. She was sick of the dug well drying up in hot weather; she wanted an artesian well.

Royal: Was she adamant?

Urban: I don't know about that, but her sister had an artesian well, so she had to have one too. Got it into her head, she just had to have an artesian well, and an in-door bathroom with a tub. Had to have it! Hired the job out and the fellas come in with their big truck and that big old thumpa-thumpa drill. They commenced to drilling. Course you had to pay by the foot, so the deeper they went, the more it cost you. You could practically see the dollar bills floating up from that hole and out of sight. They drilled down about two-hundred feet, just a-grinning, 'till they drilled into a mess of mica. Course it was soft, and they didn't realize until the whole thing caved in on itself. The thumpa-thumpa got buried. They couldn't extract it, couldn't afford to leave it. Had to bring in the derricks and pulleys and earth movers and so forth—to dig out what they lost on the first pass. By God, if they didn't drill right into that pocket of mica again, and lose that bunch, too. It was some mess I'll tell you. And there was no way Mother and I were going to shell out for that debacle.

Royal: Did your mother ever get her artesian, Urban?

Urban: Just kept bringing in more equipment and losing it down the hole—tractors, bulldozers, cranes, bigger cranes. You ever see that ship-moving crane up to Bath Ironworks—well it wa'n't that big but pretty close. The hole got bigger and bigger. Pretty soon the barn slid in. Pretty soon the house slid in. Mother and I had to sell off the land and move. They used to call that part of town West Woodford.

Royal: I heard of North, South, and East Woodford. But no West Woodford. There is no West Woodford, Urban.

Urban: Not any more there isn't. It's all down in the hole.

Puddings, Custards & other Desserts

"Gothick" Style

"Gothick" Style

In 1819, the New Hampshire Legislature voted in the Toleration Act. This meant that citizens were no longer required to pay taxes to support the state's Congregational churches. Nine years later, St. Andrew's Episcopal Church was built in Hopkinton Village out of stone quarried in the town. It was built in a "Gothick" style, which predated the Victorian neo-Gothic craze by quite a few years. This picture is of a stained glass window in that church.

Close by the site where the church stands, there took place a quick, but historic, event on June 27, 1825. On that day, General Lafayette made a stop during his tour of the United States fifty years after the American Revolution began. Lafayette, who had been only 19 when he came to America to serve with George Washington, was one of the few leading figures of the Revolution still alive in 1825. As the man who had helped convince France to support the American cause and who had risked his own life in service to America, this French aristocrat was also considered a great hero himself. He was mobbed like a modern rock star everywhere he went, and souveniers bearing his name and face sold like hotcakes all over the United States.

After a huge reception in Concord, and a side trip to Maine, Lafayette started off for Vermont. His way led through Hopkinton. Unfortunately, he couldn't stop here long. He did pause long enough in front of the Wiggins Tavern, close to the site of this church, to shake hands with townspeople, with school children dismissed from school for the occasion, and with surviving veterans from among the more than a hundred Hopkinton men who fought in the Revolution.

SANDY STRANG

Sandy Strang graduated from The Massachusetts College of Art where she majored in commercial and advertising design. She has worked as a freelance artist and has given private art lessons. Her concentration is in pen and ink renderings, and pastel and charcoal drawings. Recently, she was pleased to have presented a large rendering of Hopkinton's St. Andrew's Church to David Souter, Supreme Court Justice. In her own work, she has crafted stone animals, and created the Riverbend Stone Menagerie.

Sherried Date Pudding

Created by Chef Joan DeBrine of Maple Hedge Bed & Breakfast
Serves 8 to 10

For the sherry mixture:
1 cup (packed) brown sugar
1/2 cup sherry
1 1/2 cups hot water
2 tablespoons butter

For the pudding:
1 cup granulated sugar
1 cup flour
2 teaspoons baking powder
1/3 cup (5 1/3 tablespoons) butter
1 cup chopped dates
1/2 cup chopped nuts
1/2 cup milk

Preheat oven to 350 degrees. Grease a 9-inch pan. In a medium saucepan, combine the brown sugar, sherry, water and butter over medium-high heat. Bring to a boil, reduce heat, and let simmer 3 minutes. Remove from heat, and set aside while you prepare the pudding. Sift the dry ingredients together. Cut in the butter until the size of small peas. Stir in the dates and nuts. Add the milk, and stir to combine thoroughly. Spread evenly in the prepared pan. Pour the hot sherry mixture on top. Bake for 50 minutes. Serve warm, with whipped cream, or ice cream, if desired.

"I discovered this recipe while living in California, where wine was so plentiful."

Baked Indian Pudding

Serves 6 to 8

1 quart plus 2 cups milk
6 tablespoons cornmeal
1 teaspoon salt
2/3 cup molasses
2 tablespoons butter
1 teaspoon ground cinnamon
1/2 teaspoon ground ginger
2 eggs, lightly beaten

Preheat oven to 325 degrees. In a medium saucepan, cook 1 quart of the milk, the cornmeal and salt over medium heat for 10 to 12 minutes, until thickened like mush. Remove from heat. Now gently stir in (in the order given) the molasses, butter, spices, eggs and 1 cup of the remaining milk. Scrape the mixture into an unbuttered 9 x 13 x 2-inch baking dish. Bake for 1 1/2 hours, and then gently pour over the remaining 1 cup cold milk; do not stir! Continue baking for 1 1/2 hours, until firm but still soft. Serve warm.

"This came from a longtime restaurant in Boothbay Harbor, named 'Blueship'. It is no longer in business, but was for many years down by the footbridge across the back part of the harbor." - *Ann Simms*

Gram's Grapenut Custard Pudding

Serves 8

1 quart whole milk

1 cup Grapenuts cereal

5 eggs

1 cup sugar

1 teaspoon ground cinnamon

1/2 teaspoon grated nutmeg

whipped cream, for serving, if desired.

Preheat oven to 350 degrees. In a medium bowl, stir together the milk and Grapenuts. Set aside to soften. In a large mixing bowl, beat the eggs and sugar until light. Beat in the cinnamon, nutmeg and the Grapenuts mixture. Pour into an ungreased 1 1/2-quart baking dish, and sprinkle with additional cinnamon and nutmeg if desired. Set the baking dish in a larger pan, and add boiling water to the pan to reach about 1/2 inch up the side of the baking dish. Bake for 1 hour, until a knife inserted into the center of the pudding comes out clean. Serve warm or cold, with whipped cream if desired.

"This recipe was given to me by a 90-year-old man who remembered this 'comfort' dessert on a cold winter's night." - *Khristin Carroll*

Steamed Pudding with Hard Sauce
Serves 16

For the pudding:
1/2 cup shortening
1 cup milk
1 cup molasses
1 cup raisins
2 cups flour
1 teaspoon baking soda
1 teaspoon grated nutmeg
1/2 teaspoon ground cloves
1 teaspoon salt

For the hard sauce:
1/2 cup (8 tablespoons) butter
1 1/2 cups confectioners' sugar
2 teaspoons vanilla extract
grated nutmeg

Prepare the pudding:
   In a large saucepan, melt the shortening, and then remove from heat. Add the milk, molasses and raisins, and set aside. In a medium bowl, combine flour, baking soda, nutmeg, cloves and salt. Add these dry ingredients to the raisin mixture, and stir to combine thoroughly.

   Grease two, 11 1/2-ounce coffee cans with plastic lids. Pour the pudding mixture into the cans, and cover tightly. Place on a rack in a steamer, and add boiling water to reach halfway up the sides of the cans. Steam the pudding for 3 hours; check occasionally that the water is continually at a boil, and add more water as needed. When done, slice the pudding 1/4 to 1/2 inch thick. Serve warm with hard sauce.

Prepare the hard sauce:
   Cream the butter until light. Gradually beat in the sugar, and then vanilla. Transfer to a serving bowl, and top with a sprinkle of nutmeg. Cover tightly and refrigerate until needed.

Crème Celeste with Raspberry Sauce

Created by Chef Laurie Tweedie of The Darby Field Inn & Restaurant

Serves 16

For the Crème Celeste:

1 pint heavy cream

3/4 cup sugar

1 tablespoon unflavored gelatin

1/2 cup cold water

1 cup sour cream

1/4 cup kirsch, brandy or Cointreau

Raspberry Sauce (below)

For the Raspberry Sauce:

2 cups fresh or thawed, frozen raspberries

2 to 3 tablespoons confectioners' sugar, to taste

juice of one lemon

For the garnish:

fresh mint sprigs or unsprayed, edible flowers such as Johnny jump-ups

Prepare the Crème Celeste:

In a small saucepan, combine the cream and sugar over medium heat. Bring just to a simmer, stirring to dissolve the sugar. Remove from heat. Sprinkle the gelatin over the cold water, and let it soften for 10 minutes. Add this to the cream mixture, and stir until dissolved. Transfer the mixture to a medium, stainless steel or glass bowl, and whisk in the sour cream and kirsch. Pour into 4-ounce ramekins or custard cups, and cover tightly. Refrigerate overnight if possible.

Prepare the Raspberry Sauce:

Pass the raspberries through a sieve. Add the sugar and lemon juice, and stir to combine well.

Unmold the Crème Celeste and garnish as desired. Serve at once with Raspberry Sauce.

Pumpkin Crème Brulée

Created by Executive Chef Joseph Peterson of the Sunset Hill House
Serves 12

For the pastry:

1 cup slivered almonds

1/4 cup (packed) brown sugar

10 sheets filo pastry

1/4 cup (4 tablespoons) butter, melted and cooled

For the custard:

12 eggs

2 cups heavy cream, scalded and cooled

1 cup boiled, peeled pumpkin or canned pumpkin purée

3/4 cup granulated sugar

Preheat oven to 350 degrees.

Prepare the pastry:

In a small bowl, combine the almonds and sugar. Place 1 sheet of filo pastry on a clean work surface, and drizzle with butter. Sprinkle lightly with the almond mixture. Cover with another sheet of filo, and repeat the layers until you have used all 10 sheets of pastry. Cut the stack into 3-inch squares, and gently transfer to a baking sheet. Bake for 5 to 7 minutes, until golden brown. Remove from oven, and let cool on a rack. Leave the oven on, and make the custard.

Prepare the custard:

In a large mixing bowl, beat the eggs and cream until smooth. Add the pumpkin and sugar, and beat well. Pour into a buttered, 13 x 9 x 2-inch baking dish. Bake for 20 to 30 minutes, until golden brown. Remove from oven, and let cool. When cool, cut into 12 squares.

To assemble: Lay one square of filo on serving dish. Place a square of custard on the filo, and cover with another square of filo.

Kahlua Tiramisu

Serves 10 to 12

For the espresso sauce:

2 teaspoons instant coffee

1 tablespoon hot water

1/4 cup Kahlua coffee liqueur

1/2 teaspoon vanilla extract

For the tiramisu:

16 ounces cream cheese, softened

3 tablespoons milk

1 cup (unsifted) confectioners' sugar

3 tablespoons Kahlua coffee liqueur

1 teaspoon vanilla extract

2 1-ounce squares semi-sweet
   chocolate, grated

1 cup heavy cream

6 ounces ladyfingers, split in half

For the topping:

1/2 cup heavy cream

1 tablespoon (unsifted) confectioners'
   sugar

1/4 teaspoon vanilla extract

Prepare the espresso sauce:

In a small bowl, stir the instant coffee in the hot water until dissolved. Stir in the liqueur and vanilla, and set aside.

Assemble the tiramisu:

In a large mixing bowl, beat the cream cheese and milk until fluffy. Beat in the sugar, liqueur and vanilla. Add the chocolate, and mix just to combine. In a small mixing bowl, whip the cream until stiff. Fold this into the cream-cheese mixture, and set aside.

Line the bottom of a 3-inch-deep oval or rectangular dish with ladyfinger halves, split side up. Brush the ladyfingers with half of the espresso sauce. Spread half of the cream-cheese mixture over the ladyfingers. Repeat with the remaining ladyfingers, espresso sauce, and cream-cheese mixture.

Prepare the topping:

In a small mixing bowl, combine the cream, sugar and vanilla. Beat until stiff. Spread over the top of the tiramisu.

Cover tightly, and refrigerate overnight. Serve with a garnish of additional grated chocolate, if desired.

Lily's Puff Pastry

Serves 10 to 12

For the dough:

1/2 cup (8 tablespoons) butter
or margarine

1 cup flour

2 tablespoons cold water

For the filling:

1/2 cup (8 tablespoons) butter
or margarine

2 teaspoons almond extract

1 cup flour

3 eggs

For the icing:

2 tablespoons butter, softened

3 ounces cream cheese, softened

2 tablespoons half-and-half or milk

1 cup confectioners' sugar

1/4 cup chopped almonds

Preheat oven to 350 degrees.

Prepare the dough:

In a medium mixing bowl, cut the butter into the flour until pea-sized. Sprinkle with the water, and stir with a fork. Knead briefly, then shape into 2 5-inch-long rolls. Using the heel of the hand, press each into a strip 12 x 3 inches, and place about 3 inches apart on a 12 x 15-inch ungreased cookie sheet.

Prepare the filling:

In a medium saucepan, bring 1 cup water and butter to a rolling boil. Remove from heat, and add almond extract and flour quickly. Use a wooden spoon to beat this smooth over very low heat.

Remove from heat, and add the eggs one at a time, beating well after each addition. Spread filling evenly over the dough strips. Bake about 40 minutes, until top is crisp and golden. Let cool.

Prepare the icing:

In a medium bowl, beat the butter, cream cheese, and half-and-half until creamy. Add the sugar, and beat until smooth. Spread over the cooled pastries, and sprinkle with nuts.

Best eaten the same day!

Rhubarb Crisp

Serves 4 to 6

3 cups rhubarb, sliced into 1-inch lengths

1 egg, beaten

3/4 cup granulated sugar

2 tablespoons flour

For the crumb topping:

1/4 cup (4 tablespoons) butter, softened

1/2 cup (packed) brown sugar

2/3 cup flour

Preheat oven to 350 degrees. Grease an 8 x 8-inch square glass baking dish. In a large bowl, stir the rhubarb with the egg to coat. Add sugar and flour, and combine well. Transfer the rhubarb to the greased baking dish. In a medium bowl, stir together the crumb topping ingredients, and sprinkle this mixture over the rhubarb. Bake for 30 minutes, or until the rhubarb is soft and bubbly.

The crisp can be eaten warm, but we think it tastes better after it has cooled to room temprature.

Classic Apple Crisp

6 servings

6 to 8 crisp apples, peeled, cored, and cut into 2-inch pieces

1 1/2 cups rolled oats

3/4 cup (packed) brown sugar

1/4 cup flour

1 1/2 teaspoon ground cinnamon

1/4 teaspoon grated nutmeg

1/4 teaspoon salt

1/2 cup (8 tablespoons) butter, softened

Preheat oven to 375 degrees. Lightly butter a 6- to 8-cup baking dish. Distribute the apples evenly in the baking dish. Put the remaining ingredients in a large plastic zip-lock bag. Press the air out, and seal the bag. Squeeze these ingredients together until well blended and crumbly. Sprinkle the crumbled mixture evenly over the apples. Bake for 40 to 60 minutes, until the topping is golden brown, and the juices begin to bubble. Let cool slightly before serving.

"My family's favorite fall treat. Serve with a scoop of ice cream or dollop of whipped cream." -*Tammy Clay*

Apple Crisp

Created by Chef Loretta Deppe of The Red Sleigh Inn Bed & Breakfast
Serves 4 to 6

4 or 5 apples, peeled and cut into
    wedges

1/2 cup raisins

1/2 cup cranberries

3/4 cup flour

1 cup sugar

1/2 cup (8 tablespoons) butter,
    melted

Preheat oven to 350 degrees. Arrange the apples in a large pie plate, and sprinkle with the raisins and cranberries. Pour one cup of water over all. In a medium bowl, stir together the flour and sugar. Add the butter, and blend together with a fork. Sprinkle the flour mixture evenly over the apples. Bake for 45 minutes to 1 hour, until the juices are bubbling, and the topping is golden brown. Serve warm, with yogurt or ice cream, if desired.

Best Blueberry Cobbler

Created by Lynda and Jim Dunwell of the Carter Notch Inn
Serves 8

2 pints (4 cups) fresh or thawed, frozen blueberries

1/2 cup seedless red raspberry jam

1 cup flour

1 tablespoon sugar

1 teaspoon baking powder

1/3 teaspoon salt

3 tablespoons cold, unsalted butter, cut into bits

1/2 cup light cream or milk

Preheat oven to 425 degrees. In a round or square, 8-inch baking dish, combine the berries and jam. In a medium bowl, stir together the flour, sugar, baking powder and salt to combine well. Cut in the butter with a pastry blender, or rub it in with your fingers, until the mixture is sandy. Add the cream, and stir with a fork to form a soft dough. Drop generous tablespoons of dough onto the berry mixture. Bake for 25 to 30 minutes, until the topping is golden brown, and the berries are bubbling around the edges. Let cool for at least 10 minutes before serving.

Strawberry-Rhubarb Cobbler

Serves 6 to 8

For the fruit:

2 cups hulled, halved strawberries

1 pound rhubarb, trimmed and cut
    into 1/2-inch pieces

1 cup sugar

1/3 cup flour

1/4 teaspoon salt

1/2 teaspoon vanilla extract

1 cup (approximately) orange juice

For the topping:

1 cup flour

1 tablespoon sugar

1 1/2 teaspoons baking powder

1/2 teaspoon salt

3 tablespoons shortening

1/2 cup milk

Prepare the Fruit:

In a large bowl, combine the strawberries, rhubarb, sugar, flour, salt and vanilla gently, but thoroughly, using a rubber spatula. Let sit for 10 minutes. Preheat oven to 350 degrees.

Transfer the fruit mixture to a large saucepan. Over medium-high heat, bring it to a boil, stirring occasionally. Remove from heat, and stir in the orange juice; do not add so much that the mixture is runny. Set this aside while you prepare the topping.

Prepare the topping:

In a medium bowl, toss together the flour, sugar, baking powder and salt. With a pastry cutter, cut in the shortening until it resembles meal. Stir in the milk to make a soft dough.

Scrape the fruit mixture into a shallow 9 x 13 x 2-inch baking dish. Drop the dough by spoonfuls to cover the fruit. Bake for 30 to 40 minutes, until the fruit is bubbly, and the topping is golden brown.

Christine's Hot Fruit Compote

Created by Chef Christine Crowe of The Crowes' Nest
Serves 10 to 12

For the fruit:

6 ounces pitted prunes, chopped

6 ounces dried apricots, chopped

3 ounces dried cranberries

1 20-ounce can pineapple chunks, undrained

1 16-ounce can mandarin orange sections, drained

1 21-ounce can cherry pie filling

1 cup vermouth or Campari

For the Mock Devonshire Cream:

1/2 cup sour cream

1/4 cup (packed) brown sugar

3 tablespoons milk

1/2 cup heavy cream

Preheat oven to 300 degrees.
Prepare the fruit:

In a 2-quart casserole, thoroughly combine all of the fruit and vermouth. Bake for 45 minutes. Spoon into individual serving dishes.

Prepare Mock Devonshire Cream:

In a small bowl, combine the sour cream, sugar and milk. In a medium bowl, whip the heavy cream. Fold the sour-cream mixture into the whipped cream. Top each fruit serving with the Mock Devonshire Cream.

This delicious Mock Devonshire Cream will keep tightly covered and refrigerated, for 3 weeks.

Apricot-Apple Compote

Created by Chef Meg Curtis of Stonewall Farm
Serves 6 to 8

8 Granny Smith apples, peeled and
    coarsely chopped
1/4 cup fresh lemon juice
1 cup dried apricots, halved
3/4 cup sugar
6 tablespoons apricot jam or jelly
grated zest of 2 lemons
2 cinnamon sticks
1/2 cup chopped walnuts
1/2 cup raisins

For the garnish:
lemon yogurt
fresh mint leaves
fresh viola or nasturtium blossoms
    (unsprayed)

In a large saucepan, combine the apples, lemon juice, apricots and 2 1/2 cups water over medium-high heat. Bring to a boil, reduce the heat, and let simmer until the fruit is tender. Using a slotted spoon, remove the fruit to a medium bowl, and set aside. Add the sugar, jam, zest and cinnamon to the cooking liquid in the saucepan. Bring to a boil, stirring constantly. Reduce the heat, and let simmer until syrupy. Pour the syrup over the fruit. Add the nuts and raisins, and toss gently. Discard the cinnamon. Serve warm, or cover tightly and refrigerate until cold. Divide the compote among small serving dishes, and garnish as desired.

"This was a recipe that I took out of a magazine years ago, and experimented until I found the right ingredients to suit our palates! I find decorating with violas, nasturtiums and mint a great final touch."

Cranberry Poached Pears

Created by Chef Barbara Holmes of Mt. Chocorua View House
Serves 6

3 cups cranberry, cran-raspberry, or
    cran-strawberry juice
1 cinnamon stick
2 whole cloves
1/2 lemon, sliced thin
3 ripe, firm pears
2 teaspoons fresh lemon juice

For the garnish:
Thin lemon slices or fresh mint sprigs

In a large saucepan, combine the cranberry juice, cinnamon, cloves and lemon slices. Bring to a slow simmer. Peel, core and quarter the pears; cut each quarter into 3 or 4 pieces. In a medium bowl, gently toss the pears with the lemon juice. Add the pears to the cranberry mixture, and let simmer very gently for about 15 minutes, until pears are just tender, stirring occasionally. Remove from heat. Using a slotted spoon, gently remove the pears from the liquid, and return them to the bowl. Strain the liquid from the saucepan over the pears. Cover tightly, and refrigerate overnight. This keeps well in the refrigerator for several days. Garnish with lemon or mint.

Poached Pears

Created by Chef Christine Crowe of The Crowes' Nest
Serves 4

10 ounces frozen berries, thawed
2 tablespoons confectioners' sugar
2 Bosc or Comice pears
1/2 cup white wine
1 1/2 teaspoons chopped fresh mint, plus 4 whole mint sprigs

In a food processor or blender, purée the berries with the sugar. Strain and discard the seeds. In a small saucepan over medium-high heat, bring the purée to a boil. Reduce the heat, and simmer until reduced to 1/2 cup (about 8 to 10 minutes). Reserve.

Peel the pears, and halve them lengthwise. Core with a melon baller or paring knife. Set each pear half, cut side down, on a cutting board. Starting 3/4 inch from the stem end, slice pear lengthwise into 1/4-inch slices, leaving the slices attached at the stem end.

Arrange the pears in a single layer in a microwave-safe dish. Pour the wine over the pears. Cover with plastic wrap, and vent. Microwave on high for 5 minutes. Baste the pears with the cooking juices, cover, and continue cooking on high until nearly tender, about 3 minutes.

Divide the reserved purée among 4 small plates. Fan the pears on the purée, and garnish with chopped mint and mint sprigs.

You may substitute 1/2 cup fruit jam for the frozen berries. Omit the sugar, thin with a little wine, and melt on top of the stove just until smooth.

Apple Fritters

Compliments of the Mount Washington Hotel
Makes 16 fritters

1 cup flour

2 teaspoons baking powder

1/4 cup sugar

1 1/2 teaspoon salt

1 egg

1/2 cup milk

2 Granny Smith apples, peeled, cored, and cut into 8 wedges

1 tablespoon butter, melted and cooled

vegetable oil, for frying

In a small bowl, sift together the flour, baking powder, sugar and salt. In a medium bowl, beat together the egg and milk. Add the flour mixture, and stir until smooth. Fold in the apple pieces and butter. In a deep-fat fryer, cook the apple pieces at 395 degrees for a few minutes, until golden brown. Drain on paper toweling, and serve hot or warm.

Frozen Raspberry Soufflé

Created by Executive Chef Jeffrey Woolley of The Manor On Golden Pond
Serves 8

16 ounces frozen raspberries
1/4 cup brandy
1 teaspoon almond extract
6 eggs, separated
1/2 cup sugar
1 cup heavy cream

Using parchment or wax paper, and rubber bands or string, make a paper collar to extend 1 inch up the sides of 8 4-ounce ramekins. Combine the raspberries, brandy and almond extract in a food processor or blender, and purée. Pass the purée through a fine-mesh strainer, and reserve; discard the seeds. In a large mixing bowl, beat the yolks with 1/4 cup of the sugar until it falls from the beaters in ribbons; set aside. In another large bowl, beat the whites until foamy. While beating, gradually add the remaining 1/4 cup sugar, and beat to stiff peaks; set aside. In a third, smaller bowl, whip the cream until stiff. First fold the raspberry mixture thoroughly into the yolk mixture, then fold in the egg-white mixture, and finally, the whipped cream.

Fill the prepared ramekins, and freeze for 8 hours. 10 minutes before serving, remove them from the freezer to soften slightly, remove the paper collar, and serve.

The Bretton Arms

Casual elegance with flair...

Built in 1896, The Bretton Arms is a designated National Historic Landmark. Amidst the splendor and serenity of New Hampshire's White Mountains, the Inn has been faithfully restored with attention to maintaining period detail. Thirty-four spacious guest rooms and suites feature private baths, in-room telephones and color cable televisions. Gourmet dinners and hearty country breakfasts are served in the intimate dining room. Just a short stroll from the grand Mount Washington Hotel, guests of the Inn are offered all the amenities of the historic Resort, including two golf courses and an 18-hole putting green situated around the Hotel's spectacular annual gardens. In the warm months, enjoy tennis, take a horseback or carriage ride, swim in the pools, or simply enjoy a stroll with a view of the magnificent Presidential Range. Winter activities abound, including nearby downhill and cross-country skiing, snowshoeing, skating, or a romantic sleigh ride. Whatever your pleasure, you'll enjoy experiencing the timeless elegance and endless recreational pursuits of this classic New England inn.

The Bretton Arms
Route 302
Bretton Woods, NH 03575
603.278.1000
800.258.0330

Honey-Thyme Ice Cream

Created by Chef de Cuisine Brian Roberge of the Bretton Arms
Makes about 1 quart

2 cups milk
2 cups heavy cream
1/2 cup honey
5 egg yolks
16 sprigs fresh thyme

In the top of a double boiler set over simmering water, combine the milk, 1 cup of the cream, the honey and the egg yolks. Cook, stirring constantly, for 10 to 15 minutes, until the mixture is thick enough to coat a spoon. Remove from heat; stir in the thyme, and let sit to infuse for 10 minutes.

Strain the mixture into a bowl, and discard the thyme sprigs. Stir the remaining 1 cup cream into the mixture, and let cool completely. Freeze the mixture in an ice-cream maker, following the manufacturer's directions.

Blueberry and Lemon Yogurt Soup

Created by Kim O'Mahoney of the Inn at Portsmouth Harbor

Serves 10

2 pints blueberries, preferably tiny
    wild Maine berries

1 1/2 cups water

3/4 cup granulated sugar

1 thinly sliced lemon, seeds removed

1 teaspoon ground cinnamon

2 cups nonfat vanilla yogurt

4 tablespoons freshly squeezed
    lemon juice

4 tablespoons confectioners' sugar

For the garnish:

edible pansies or Johnnie jump-ups
    (unsprayed)

In a medium saucepan, combine the berries, water, the granulated sugar, lemon and cinnamon over medium-high heat. Bring to a boil, reduce the heat, and let simmer for 15 minutes. Remove from the heat, and let cool. Process the mixture in a blender until smooth. Transfer the mixture to a medium bowl, cover tightly, and refrigerate overnight, or for at least several hours.

Combine the yogurt, lemon juice and confectioners' sugar. Whisk this into the blueberry mixture. Ladle the soup into serving bowls, and garnish.

Cantaloupe Yogurt Soup

Created by Kim O'Mahoney of the Inn at Portsmouth Harbor

Serves 6-8

1 very ripe cantaloupe, peeled,
    seeded, and cut into chunks

1/2 cup orange juice

2 tablespoons sugar

8 ounces nonfat vanilla yogurt

For the garnish:

fresh mint sprigs

Combine the cantaloupe, juice and sugar in a blender container, and purée. Transfer the mixture to a medium mixing bowl, and whisk in the yogurt. Cover tightly, and refrigerate until cold. Ladle the soup into serving bowls, garnish, and serve at once. The soup can be prepared the day before; whisk well before serving.

Put either soup in an ice-cream maker to make great frozen yogurt!

Cookies & Sweets

Revere Bell

Revere Bell

Although it looks serene in this picture, Hopkinton's First Congregational Church has seen its share of turbulence. When the original land grant was made to town founders in 1735, part of the bargain was that they must organize and build a church in short order. Hopkinton's early settlers came from Massachusetts Colony, staunchly Puritan in tradition, where church and government were closely connected. Therefore, the First Church, when built, would not only be the public Meetinghouse, but town officers would hire and fire its ministers, as well as pay them from tax coffers.

Hopkinton's First Church/Meetinghouse, however, took quite a while to materialize. Although the church was formally organized in 1757, construction was delayed, not only by Indian raids and the French and Indian Wars, but also by fiery disagreement as to where it should be situated. Finally, in 1766, a church was built near what is now the village green — across the road from the one pictured here.

On February 5, 1789, that original church met a blazing end under highly questionable circumstances. One would have thought that the presence in front of the church of a pair of stocks and a whipping post would have deterred such a crime. Two local men were "gaoled" — and later "forgiven" — for torching the building. Church historian Steve Thomas, however, believes that an unstable young man who burned down a couple of barns in Amherst (and perhaps its courthouse, too) might have been the culprit in Hopkinton as well. He never was suspected or questioned by the investigating Selectmen.

The present church, built right after the fire, originally faced a different direction. As part of an 1830s remodeling, the church was rotated 90 degrees by teams of oxen. The steeple, added in 1809, houses an 1811 Revere bell (cast during Paul Revere's lifetime), which still tolls the hours.

(Please refer to page 148 for information on André Hurtgen).

Chocolate Chews

Created by Chef Becky Mallar of The 1785 Inn & Restaurant
Makes 3 dozen

4 eggs

2 cups granulated sugar

2 teaspoons vanilla extract

5 ounces unsweetened chocolate, melted and cooled

1/2 cup (8 tablespoons) butter, melted and cooled

2 cups flour

2 teaspoons baking powder

1 teaspoon salt

1/2 cup chopped nuts (optional)

confectioners' sugar, for rolling

In a large mixing bowl, beat the eggs with the sugar and vanilla. Gradually beat in the chocolate and butter. In a medium bowl, thoroughly combine the flour, baking powder and salt. Add this to the chocolate mixture, and beat until all ingredients are thoroughly mixed. Add the nuts, if desired. Cover the dough tightly, and refrigerate for several hours or overnight.

Preheat oven to 350 degrees. Grease cookie sheets. Shape the dough into 1 1/2-inch balls, and roll them in confectioners' sugar. Place the cookies 3 inches apart on the prepared sheets, and bake for 10 to 15 minutes, to desired doneness. For a soft cookie center, remove from the oven while the cookies are still soft in the center.

"If you are a chocolate lover, this cookie is for you. It has always been one of my family's favorites. It is a moist, dense chocolate dough that absolutely melts in your mouth. Each February, the Mount Washington Ski Touring Association sponsors a chocolate festival where people ski to various businesses along the trail to sample all of the chocolate treats offered by each of the participating properties. Along with several other delectable chocolate treats, we always offer chocolate chews. They are fun to make, great to look at, and even more enjoyable to eat."

Mocha Fudge Cookies

Makes 6 1/2 dozen

3/4 cup (12 tablespoons) butter

4 ounces unsweetened chocolate, chopped

3 1/2 cups semisweet chocolate chips

2 tablespoons instant coffee

4 eggs

1 3/4 cups sugar

2 teaspoons vanilla extract

1 1/2 cups flour

1 teaspoon baking soda

1 cup chopped peanuts

Silpat baking mat or parchment paper

Preheat oven to 350 degrees. In a heavy saucepan over low heat, or in a microwave-safe container in a microwave oven, melt the butter, unsweetened chocolate, and 1 1/2 cups of the chocolate chips, stirring occasionally until smooth. Stir in the instant coffee, and set aside. In a large mixing bowl, beat the eggs, sugar and vanilla until thick. Stir in the flour and baking soda until thoroughly combined. Add the chocolate mixture, the remaining 2 cups chocolate chips, and the peanuts, and stir to incorporate well.

Drop the batter by tablespoons onto an air-bake cookie sheet lined with a silpat baking mat or parchment paper (not a greased pan). Bake for 8 to 9 minutes; do not overbake. The cookies will look crinkled. Remove from oven, and cool for 1 to 2 minutes. Using a spatula, transfer the cookies to a wire rack to cool completely. Store in an air-tight container. If the cookies are not to be eaten within a few days, tightly wrap and freeze them.

"I have found that air-bake cookie sheets with silpat mats work best with this recipe. This recipe was created for my husband, Craig, who loves cookies, especially anything chocolate. (He thinks the major food groups are chocolate, butter, sugar and heavy cream!!) Very fudgy." - *Linda Dunning*

Mocha Stars

Makes 50 to 60 2-inch cookies

1/2 cup (8 tablespoons) butter, softened

1/2 cup (packed) light brown sugar

2 teaspoons finely ground espresso roast coffee beans, sifted

2 teaspoons unsweetened cocoa powder

dash of salt

1 egg yolk

1 tablespoon coffee liqueur

1 1/2 cups flour

3/4 cups semisweet chocolate chips

1 tablespoon vegetable shortening

In a medium mixing bowl, beat the butter on high speed for 30 seconds. Add the sugar, coffee, cocoa and salt, and continue beating until well combined, scraping the sides of the bowl occasionally. Beat in the egg yolk and liqueur thoroughly. Use the mixer to beat in as much flour as possible, and then use a wooden spoon to stir in any remaining flour. Divide the dough in half and pat each half into a disk. Cover tightly and chill for about 4 hours, or until the dough is easy to handle.

Preheat oven to 350 degrees. On a lightly floured surface, roll out one of the disks of dough to 1/8- to 1/4-inch thickness. Using a star-shaped cookie cutter, cut out cookies, and place them 1 inch apart on an ungreased cookie sheet. Bake for about 8 minutes, or until the tops look dry. Remove from oven and leave on the cookie sheet for 1 minute. Transfer the cookies to a wire rack to finish cooling. Repeat the process using the rest of the dough. In a heavy, small saucepan, combine the chocolate chips and shortening over medium-low heat, and stir until melted. Dip some of the cookie star points into the melted chocolate. Set the dipped cookies on wax paper to dry.

Kargatton Kisses

Makes 2 dozen kisses

2 egg whites
3/4 cup sugar
1 cup semisweet chocolate chips
1 cup chopped nuts
brown paper or parchment paper

Preheat oven to 350 degrees. In the small or medium bowl of an electric mixer, beat egg whites and sugar until very stiff. Fold in chocolate and nuts. Drop by teaspoons onto brown paper, and set in the oven. Turn off the heat, and leave overnight until cold.

Valley Farm's Very Best Chocolate Chip Cookie

Created by Chef Jacqueline Badders of the Inn at Valley Farms
Makes 1 1/2 to 2 1/2 dozen cookies

2/3 cup (11 tablespoons) butter, softened

1 egg

1/2 teaspoon vanilla extract

1/2 cup granulated sugar

1/2 cup (packed) brown sugar

1/4 teaspoon salt

1 teaspoon baking soda

1 2/3 cup sifted flour

1/2 cup sweetened, flaked coconut

1/2 cup chopped pecans

8 ounces semisweet chocolate chips

Preheat oven to 375 degrees. In a medium mixing bowl, combine the butter, egg, vanilla, 1/2 teaspoon water, both sugars, salt and baking soda. Mix at medium speed until blended. Add the flour, and mix until well blended. Add the coconut, pecans and chocolate chips. Drop the dough onto lightly greased cookie sheets. Bake for approximately 12 minutes, until golden brown. Remove to a wire rack to cool.

"A family favorite for years before we opened our bed and breakfast, now our guests' favorite, too! I usually double this recipe, then freeze any extra dough so that I can bake fresh cookies at the drop of a hat."

Coriander Cookies

Makes 36 2-inch cookies

3/4 cup (12 tablespoons) margarine
  or butter, softened

1 cup sugar

1 egg, at room temperature

1 tablespoon milk

1 teaspoon vanilla extract

2 tablespoons ground coriander

2 cups flour

Preheat oven to 400 degrees. In a medium mixing bowl, cream the margarine and sugar until light. Beat in the egg, and then the remaining ingredients. Shape the dough into 1/2-inch balls, and place on ungreased cookie sheets. Flatten each ball with a fork. Bake for 8 to 10 minutes, until golden.

Pumpkin Cookies

Makes 3 to 4 dozen, depending on size

1 cup (16 tablespoons) butter or margarine

1 cup (packed) brown sugar

1 cup granulated sugar

1 egg

1 teaspoon vanilla extract

1 cup cooked pumpkin, winter squash, sweet potato, yam or carrot

2 cups flour

1 cup quick-cooking oats

1 teaspoon baking soda

1 teaspoon ground cinnamon, pumpkin pie spice or apple pie spice

1/2 teaspoon salt

1 cup raisins, dried cranberries or dried cherries

parchment paper

Preheat oven to 350 degrees. Cream butter and sugars. Beat in egg and vanilla, then add pumpkin, and continue beating until thoroughly combined. Add the dry ingredients, and mix well. Stir in dried fruit. If you have time, cover the dough tightly, and refrigerate for 1 to 2 hours. (This is not absolutely necessary.)

Drop dough by tablespoons onto cookie sheets lined with parchment paper. Bake for 20 to 25 minutes, until the cookies are slightly crisp outside, but still soft inside. Let cool completely, then store in an air-tight plastic container with plastic wrap or wax paper between layers of cookies.

Old-Fashioned Molasses Cookies

Makes 4 to 5 dozen

3 cups flour

1/2 cup sugar

1 teaspoon salt

1 teaspoon baking soda

1 teaspoon baking powder

1 1/2 teaspoon ground ginger

1/2 teaspoon ground cloves

2 1/2 teaspoons ground cinnamon

3/4 cup vegetable shortening, melted and cooled

1 egg

1 12-ounce jar Grandma's brand molasses

Preheat oven to 375 degrees. Grease cookie sheets. In a large mixing bowl, combine the ingredients in the order given. Drop the dough by tablespoons onto the prepared sheets, about 2 inches apart. Bake for 10 minutes — underdone is better.

"A wonderful after-school treat with milk (Nanny's special) passed on from Sallie Hemingway, a dear friend from Hopkinton who is now living in Maine. The secret is in the baking." -*Ruthie White*

Grandma Bruno's Brown Sugar Rocks

Makes 3 to 4 dozen cookies

1 cup vegetable shortening

1 1/2 cups (packed) dark brown sugar

3 eggs

2 3/4 cups flour

1/2 teaspoon salt

1 heaping teaspoon ground cinnamon

1 teaspoon baking soda, dissolved in 3 teaspoons boiling water

1 cup raisins

1 cup chopped nuts

Preheat oven to 450 degrees. Grease cookie sheets. In a medium bowl, cream the shortening and sugar until light. Add the eggs, and mix well. Add the flour, salt and cinnamon, and mix well. Add the dissolved baking soda, and mix well. Stir in the raisins and nuts. Drop the dough by table-spoons onto the prepared cookie sheets, and flatten slightly. Bake for 10 minutes, until golden.

"Grandma Bruno is my grandmother's mother from Alden, MN but my grand-mother spent many a summer at my grandfather's family's farm in Epsom NH, where she became quite well known for these cookies." - *Susan Yonkers*

Christmas Thumbprint Cookies

Created by Chef Laurie Tweedie of The Darby Field Inn & Restaurant
Makes 2 to 3 dozen

1/4 cup (packed) brown sugar

1/4 cup vegetable shortening

1/4 cup (4 tablespoons)margarine or
butter, softened

1/2 teaspoon vanilla extract

1 egg yolk

1 cup flour

1/4 teaspoon salt

1 cup finely chopped nuts

About 1/4 cup each strawberry
and mint jelly

Preheat oven to 350 degrees. In a medium mixing bowl, combine the brown sugar, shortening, margarine, vanilla and egg yolk, and beat until smooth. Add the flour and salt, and stir until the dough holds together. Shape into 1-inch balls, and roll in nuts. Place about 1 inch apart on ungreased cookie sheets. Press your thumb deeply into the center of each. Bake for about 10 minutes, until light brown. Remove from oven, and let cool. Fill thumbprints with strawberry or mint jelly.

Marvelous Macaroons

Makes about 2 1/2 dozen cookies

2 2/3 cups sweetened, flaked coconut
2/3 cup sugar
1/4 cup flour
1/4 teaspoon salt
4 egg whites
1 teaspoon vanilla extract
1 cup sliced almonds

Preheat oven to 325 degrees. Grease cookie sheets. In a medium bowl, combine the coconut, sugar, flour and salt thoroughly. Add the egg whites and vanilla, and stir to combine well. Stir in the almonds. Drop the dough by teaspoons onto the prepared cookie sheets. Bake for 20 to 25 minutes, until the edges and bottoms are golden brown. Remove from baking sheet immediately, and let cool on racks. Store in an airtight container for several days.

Grandmother's Oatmeal Cookies

Makes 2 1/2 dozen

1 cup canola oil
1 cup (packed) brown sugar
1 cup granulated sugar
2 eggs
2 tablespoons water
1 teaspoon vanilla extract
1 1/2 cups flour
1 teaspoon baking soda
1 teaspoon salt
3 cups rolled oats
1 cup raisins or chopped nuts

Preheat oven to 375 degrees. In a large mixing bowl, beat the oil, sugars, eggs, water and vanilla until well blended. Sift together the flour, baking soda and salt; add this to the mixing bowl, and mix well. Stir in the oats and raisins or nuts. Drop the dough by tablespoons onto ungreased cookie sheets. Bake for 8 minutes; the cookies will not look quite done, but remove them from the oven, and let them sit on the cookie sheet for a minute or two, which will make them chewier.

Peanut Butter Cookies

Makes 24 to 32 cookies

1 cup (packed) brown sugar
1 cup granulated sugar
1 cup vegetable shortening
1 cup peanut butter
2 eggs
1 teaspoon vanilla extract
3 cups flour
1 teaspoon baking soda
1/8 teaspoon salt

Preheat oven to 375 degrees. In a large mixing bowl, cream the sugars and shortening until light and fluffy. Add the peanut butter, eggs and vanilla, and mix to combine. In a medium bowl, sift together the flour, baking soda and salt. Add the flour mixture to the peanut butter mixture, and stir to combine thoroughly. Using a large spoon or ice-cream scoop, drop the dough onto ungreased cookie sheets, 2 inches apart. Press the dough balls down to 1/2 to 3/4-inch thick, using a fork criss-cross fashion. Bake for 12 minutes, until lightly golden around the edges.

Toffee Shortbread

Makes 24 bars

For the shortbread layer:
1/2 cup (8 tablespoons) butter, softened
1/3 cup sugar
1 1/3 cups flour

For the toffee layer:
1/4 cup (4 tablespoons) butter
1/4 cup sugar
3 tablespoons light corn syrup
2/3 cup sweetened condensed milk
1/2 teaspoon vanilla extract

For the topping:
3/4 cup semi-sweet chocolate chips
1/4 cup chopped, toasted almonds

Prepare the shortbread:
Preheat oven to 350 degrees. In a medium mixing bowl, cream the butter and sugar until light and fluffy. Add the flour, and continue mixing until crumbly. Press into an ungreased 9 x 13-inch pan. Bake for 20 to 25 minutes, until golden.

Prepare the toffee:
In a medium saucepan, combine the butter, sugar, corn syrup and condensed milk over medium heat. Stirring constantly, keep the mixture at a boil for 5 minutes. (There will be some browned bits of toffee.) Remove from heat, and add the vanilla. Pour the toffee over the baked shortbread, and use a spatula to spread it quickly into an even layer. Let cool at room temperature for 30 minutes to 1 hour.

Prepare the topping:
Melt the chocolate chips, and spread over the toffee. Sprinkle with almonds, and press them lightly into the chocolate. Let cool completely at room temperature before cutting.

Fig Squares

Makes 36 squares

1/2 pound dried figs
1 cup sugar
dash of salt
1 tablespoon butter
pastry for a 9-inch, double-crust pie

Preheat oven to 400 degrees. Trim and discard any stems from the figs. Mash or finely chop the figs, and put them in a medium saucepan with the sugar, 1 cup water and the salt. Cook slowly over medium-low heat until the mixture thickens. Remove from heat, add the butter, and stir until melted. Let cool slightly.

On a baking sheet with low sides (1/2 inch or so high), roll out half of the pastry to a thickness of about 1/4 inch. Evenly spread it with the fig filling right up to the edges. On a pastry board, roll out the remaining pastry to cover the filling, and gently transfer to the baking sheet. Bake for 30 to 35 minutes; do not allow to brown too much. Remove from oven, and transfer to a rack to cool. Cut into squares.

Welsh Cakes

Makes 18 to 20 3-inch cakes

3 cups flour
2 teaspoons baking powder
1/4 teaspoon salt
1 cup sugar
1 cup raisins
3/4 cup (12 tablespoons) margarine
3 eggs
up to 1/4 cup milk

In a large bowl, combine the dry ingredients and the raisins. Using your hands or a pastry blender, rub or cut in the margarine thoroughly. In a medium bowl, beat the eggs lightly with 1 tablespoon of the milk. Add the egg mixture to the flour mixture, and stir until a moist dough forms. You want the dough to hold together, but not be too sticky or too dry; add more flour or milk if needed. On a floured work surface, roll the dough 1/2 inch thick. Using a fluted tart or biscuit cutter, cut out the Welsh cakes. Gather the dough scraps into a ball, and roll out again and again, until all the dough is used. Meanwhile, heat an ungreased, nonstick frying pan (electric works best). When it is hot, cook the cakes in batches, turning once, until golden brown on both sides.

These cakes freeze well, and are great lunchbox treats. They are also wonderful with tea or coffee.

Peanut Butter Fudge

Makes 40 1 1/2-inch squares

2 cups (packed) light brown sugar
2 cups granulated sugar
2/3 cup whole milk
1 12-ounce jar peanut butter
1 7 1/2-ounce jar marshmallow fluff

Butter a 9 x 13-inch pan. In a medium saucepan, combine the sugars and milk over medium heat. Stirring constantly, keep the mixture at a rolling boil for exactly 2 1/2 minutes. Remove from heat, and quickly stir in the peanut butter and marshmallow fluff. Beat with a wooden spoon until smooth, and then quickly pour into the buttered pan. Let cool completely before cutting.

"This is a family recipe from Maine. It is quick, easy and delicious. It is a holiday favorite!" - *Michelle Bickford*
Note: The amount of peanut butter and marshmallow fluff need not be exact.

The Inn at East Hill Farm

Offering farm vacations for families since 1945

Located at the base of Mount Monadnock in the tranquil, southwestern corner of New Hampshire, the Inn at East Hill Farm maintains its tradition as a destination resort where families and friends can meet in a relaxed atmosphere that promotes true re-creation. Rooms are available in the main building, and in any of several modern and well-appointed cottages. Wholesome and delicious meals are home-cooked and served family style. Specialties include homemade breads, cookies, fritters and hearty country breakfasts. Youngsters may enjoy the adventure of collecting the eggs they eat for breakfast. No matter what the season, there is always something to do at the farm: swimming indoors or outdoors, boating, fishing, hiking, horseback riding, water skiing, hay or sleigh rides, Nordic skiing or ice skating. And when vigorous activity is not on your agenda, there are plenty of comfortable and inviting spaces for reading a good book or having a quiet conversation. Activities are planned specifically for children as well, crafts, campfires and games among them. Children may also have a chance to milk a cow and to help feed the farm animals.

The Inn at East Hill Farm
460 Monadnock
Troy, NH 03465
603.242-6495
800.242-6495
Owners Dave and Sally Adams

Mark's Brownies

Created by Chef Mark Drury of The Inn at East Hill Farm
Serves 18-24

1 1/4 cups (20 tablespoons) butter, softened

2 1/2 cups sugar

2 teaspoons vanilla extract

5 eggs

1 1/4 cups flour

2/3 cup unsweetened cocoa

2/3 cup semi-sweet chocolate chips

Preheat oven to 375 degrees. Butter a 13 x 9 x 2-inch baking dish. In a large mixing bowl, cream the butter, sugar and vanilla until light and fluffy. Add the eggs one at a time, beating well after each addition. With the mixer on low speed, gradually add the flour; mix until thoroughly blended. Gradually add the cocoa, mixing thoroughly. Using a rubber spatula, fold in the chocolate chips. Spread the batter in the prepared pan. Bake for 30 to 40 minutes, until a toothpick inserted near the center comes out clean. (For cakey, rather than fudgy, brownies, let bake for an additional 5 to 10 minutes.) Remove from oven, and let stand for 10 minutes before cutting. Serve with ice cream.

Graham Cracker Brownies

Makes 12 to 16 bars

20 to 22 graham crackers (2 of the 3
    packages in a 1-pound box)

6 ounces chocolate chips (regular or
    miniature)

1 14-ounce can sweetened
    condensed milk

1 teaspoon vanilla extract

Preheat oven to 350 degrees. Lightly grease an 8 x 8-inch or 9 x 9-inch baking pan. Seal the graham crackers in a plastic bag and crush with a rolling pin. Transfer the crumbs to a medium bowl, add the remaining ingredients, and combine well. The dough will be very stiff. Spread the dough in the prepared pan. Bake for 30 minutes. Let cool no longer than 5 to 10 minutes before cutting into bars, or they will be very hard.

Breads

The William H. Long Memorial Building

The William H. Long Memorial

Just before the Civil War, three young men — George Crowell, a farmer and shoemaker, Darwin Blanchard, a village schoolteacher, and Silas Ketcham, a store clerk — set out to preserve Hopkinton's artifacts and documents that illustrated the town's early history. Still in their 20's, these three were witnessing huge shifts in the way people lived, not only in Hopkinton but further afield.

The traditional way of life, based on farming and local commerce carried on in more or less rural isolation, was being fundamentally altered, as the revolution of that day — the industrial revolution — was taking hold. Rather than simply embracing these changes, however, Crowell, Blanchard and Ketcham banded together to found the Philomathic ("love of learning") Club, to improve its members' minds, and to preserve their town's history.

To this end, the three began collecting artifacts, documents, minerals and "curiosities" such as a "Hair Snake and her young." They also wrote about their finds in journals of the day. Over the years, the club grew in membership, eventually accepting women as well. In 1875 it was incorporated as The New Hampshire Philomathic and Antiquarian Society, which eventually became simply the New Hampshire Antiquarian Society.

The collection expanded until it outgrew the space available for housing it. Luckily, in 1890, Lucia Rollins Long offered to pay for a building as a memorial to her late husband, Hopkinton native William Harrison Long, a distinguished educator with thrifty habits. The result was the red brick (therefore somewhat fire-resistant) Long Memorial Building, still the repository and museum for this historical society founded by three young men who looked backward as well as forward.

TAMARA CRAIG

For Tamara Craig, visual art is story-telling at its most profound. She has been an artist since childhood. Awarded her BFA, she traveled through Europe to study master artists at length. Back home she continued her studies in art education in Philadelphia. She has enjoyed working as a docent in art centers and as a commercial artist. Today, she pursues her love of art through drawings, illustrations and etchings.

Oatmeal Scones

Created by Chef Joan DeBrine of Maple Hedge Bed & Breakfast
Serves 8

1 1/4 cups flour
1/2 teaspoon baking soda
1 teaspoon baking powder
1/3 cup sugar
1/2 cup (8 tablespoons) butter or margarine
1 cup oats
1/3 cup buttermilk

Preheat oven to 375 degrees. Grease a baking sheet. In a medium bowl, combine the flour, baking soda, baking powder, sugar and butter with a pastry blender until crumbly. Stir in the oats. Add the buttermilk, and stir until a soft dough forms. On the prepared baking sheet, pat the dough into a 10-inch circle. Using a serrated knife, score the dough into 8 wedges. Bake for 20 minutes, until golden brown.

"I devised this recipe from a combination of two others. The dry ingredients can be mixed ahead and refrigerated until needed."

Atwood Inn Breakfast Scones

Created by Chef Sandi Hoffmeister of the Maria Atwood Inn
Makes 10 to 12 scones

2 1/4 cups flour

1/2 cup sugar

2 teaspoons baking powder

1/2 teaspoon baking soda

1/4 teaspoon salt

1/2 cup butter-flavored vegetable
shortening

1/2 cup buttermilk

1 egg

1 teaspoon flavoring extract (vanilla,
orange or maple)

1/2 cup chopped nuts (walnuts,
pecans or hazelnuts)

1/2 cup fruit (blueberries, cranberries,
chopped dates or raisins)

(if using only nuts or fruit alone, use 1
cup total)

Preheat oven to 350 degrees. In a medium bowl, stir together the dry ingredients. Cut in the shortening. Add the buttermilk, egg, and flavoring, and stir well. Fold in the nuts and/or fruit. Knead to fully mix the ingredients. Shape the dough into a ball, and place it on a cookie sheet or baking stone. Score into 8 wedges with serrated knife. Bake for 18 to 22 minutes, until lightly browned, and a toothpick inserted near the center comes out dry.

Serve warm with butter, honey, jam or flavored cream cheese.

"Best scones in the world," said a guest from the Netherlands. If using only nuts or fruit alone, use 1 cup total.

Atwood Inn Blueberry Muffins

Created by Chef Sandi Hoffmeister of the Maria Atwood Inn
Makes 12 muffins

2 cups flour

1/2 cup granulated sugar

2 1/2 teaspoons baking powder

1/2 teaspoon salt

1/2 cup butter-flavored vegetable
shortening

1 cup buttermilk

1 egg

1 teaspoon vanilla extract

1 cup fresh or frozen blueberries

cinnamon sugar or confectioners'
sugar, for dusting

Preheat oven to 375 degrees. Grease 12 muffin cups. In a large bowl, stir together the flour, granulated sugar, baking powder and salt. Cut in the shortening. Add the buttermilk, egg and vanilla, and stir well. Fold in the blueberries, but do not overmix. Divide the batter among the muffin cups. Dust with cinnamon sugar. Bake for 15 to 20 minutes, until golden brown. Serve warm.

Useful Streusel

Created by Chef Ann Carlsmith of the Stepping Stones Bed & Breakfast
Makes about 4 cups (more with nuts)

1 cup (16 tablespoons) unsalted
butter

2 cups flour (King Arthur brand
prefered)

2 cups (packed) brown sugar

4 teaspoons ground cinnamon
(China Cassia preferred)

1 freshly grated, medium nutmeg

Optional: Chopped pecans or
walnuts, quantity as desired

Use a pastry blender to combine the ingredients until crumbly. Or, process briefly in a food processor until crumbly.

"I find a supply of streusel, always on hand, is endlessly useful at my bed and breakfast. Use this recipe as topping for muffins, coffeecakes and quick breads. Great as top crusts for fruit pies and cheesecakes, or for last-minute fruit 'crisps.' Keeps a month or longer, refrigerated in a well-sealed jar."

Rhubarb Muffins

Created by Chef Bonnie Webb of The Inn on Golden Pond
Makes 20 muffins

1 1/4 cups (packed) brown sugar
1 egg
1/2 cup vegetable oil
2 teaspoons vanilla extract
1 cup sour milk
1 1/2 cups diced rhubarb
2 1/2 cups flour
1 teaspoon baking soda
1 teaspoon baking powder
1/2 teaspoon salt

For the topping:
1 tablespoon butter, melted
1/3 cup granulated sugar
2 teaspoons ground cinnamon

Preheat oven to 400 degrees. Grease 2 sets of muffin tins. In a large mixing bowl, combine the brown sugar, egg, oil, vanilla and sour milk, and beat until well combined. Stir in the rhubarb. In a separate bowl, stir together the flour, baking soda, baking powder and salt. Add the dry ingredients to the milk mixture, and stir just until blended. Fill the prepared muffin tins 2/3 full. In a small bowl, combine the topping ingredients. Sprinkle the mixture over the batter, and bake for 20 to 25 minutes, until a toothpick inserted near the center comes out clean.

Lemon-Lime Muffins

Created by Chef Mimi Atwood of The Benjamin Prescott Inn
Makes 24 muffins

1 cup (8 tablespoons) butter, softened or melted

1 1/2 cups sugar

4 eggs

2 teaspoons lemon extract

2 1/2 cups flour

1 1/2 teaspoons baking powder

1 teaspoon salt

4 1/2 ounces (1/2 cup plus 1 tablespoon) lime juice

2 teaspoons grated lemon or lime zest

8 ounces lime yogurt

Additional lime juice (about 1/4 cup) and sugar, for dipping

Preheat oven to 350 degrees. Place paper liners in 24 muffin cups. In a large mixing bowl, cream the butter and sugar until smooth. Add the eggs, and beat well. Beat in the lemon extract. Sift together the flour, baking powder and salt. Add this to the egg mixture, alternating with the lime juice, mixing thoroughly after each addition. Fold in the zest and the yogurt.

Fill the muffin cups about 3/4 full. Bake for 20 to 30 minutes, until a toothpick inserted in the center of a muffin comes out clean.

Remove from oven, and let cool for about 15 minutes. Dip the top of each muffin in lime juice, and then in granulated sugar to coat.

Caraway Cheese Muffins
Makes 12 muffins

1 3/4 cups flour
1/4 cup sugar
2 1/2 teaspoons baking powder
1/2 teaspoon salt
3/4 cup milk
1/3 cup vegetable oil
1 egg
1 1/2 teaspoons caraway seeds
3/4 cup shredded Cheddar cheese

Preheat oven to 400 degrees. Lightly grease a 12-cup muffin tin. In a large mixing bowl, stir together the flour, sugar, baking powder and salt until well combined. In a small bowl, whisk together the milk, oil and egg. Add the milk mixture to the dry ingredients, and stir just until combined. Add the caraway seeds and cheese, and stir well. Divide the batter among the prepared muffin tins. Bake for 20 to 25 minutes, until a toothpick inserted near the center comes out clean.

Never-Fail Popovers
Makes 6 popovers

2 eggs
1 cup milk
1 tablespoon vegetable oil
1 cup flour
1/2 tablespoon salt

Preheat oven to 425 degrees. Lightly grease 6 popover cups with oil. In a blender, combine the eggs and milk and blend thoroughly. Add the oil, and blend to combine. Add the flour and salt, and blend until smooth, about 15 seconds. Divide the batter equally among cups (each will hold just under 1/2 cup batter). Bake on the middle oven rack for 30 minutes. Don't open the oven door! Let cool in cups.

Big, Brown, Antlered and Lumbering or . . . .

In Gorham, I asked third graders to describe a moose. Their response: "Delicious."

Blueberry Hot Bread

Makes 2 loaves

2 eggs

1 cup sugar

1 cup milk

1/4 cup (4 tablespoons) butter,
    melted and cooled

3 cups flour, sifted

1 teaspoon salt

4 teaspoons baking powder

2 cups blueberries (thawed if frozen)

Preheat the oven to 350 degrees. Generously grease two 8 x 4 x 2-inch baking pans. In a medium mixing bowl, beat the eggs and sugar until light. Add the milk and butter, and combine well. Sift together the flour, salt and baking powder, and add to the egg mixture. Beat just until combined. (Do not beat until smooth.) Toss the blueberries in a little extra flour; this will help keep them from sinking to the bottom of the bread. Stir them into the batter.

Divide the batter among the two baking pans. Bake for 1 hour, or until a toothpick inserted near the center comes out dry.

Pumpkin Bread

Makes 10 mini loaves

1 1/2 cups sugar
1 1/2 cups flour
1/2 teaspoon baking powder
1/2 teaspoon salt
1 teaspoon baking soda
1/2 teaspoon grated nutmeg
1/2 teaspoon ground cinnamon
1/4 teaspoon ground allspice
1/2 cup vegetable oil
1/2 cup water
1 cup canned pumpkin
2 eggs, slightly beaten

Preheat oven to 350 degrees. Prepare two, 9 x 5 x 3-inch or 10 miniature loaf pans, spraying them with baking spray, or using butter and flour. In a medium mixing bowl, combine the dry ingredients thoroughly. In a large mixing bowl, combine the wet ingredients thoroughly. Add the dry ingredients to the wet ingredients, and mix well. Divide the batter among the prepared pans. Bake mini loaves for about 30 minutes, large loaves for about an hour, until a toothpick inserted in the center comes out clean. Cool on rack for 10 minutes, then unmold and cool completely on rack.

Eastman Inn Bed & Breakfast

Your Romantic and Elegant Home Away From Home

The Eastman Inn, built in 1777 by the Noah Eastman family, is a classic three-story Georgian Colonial home complete with a wrap-around veranda. The Inn has been restored and tastefully decorated to retain the warmth and charm of the eighteenth century. The Inn has quiet surroundings and panoramic views of the mountains in all directions, and is open throughout the year. Guests are offered a full country breakfast, private baths, in-room color TV, a fireplaced living room and tastefully decorated guest rooms. The Inn is located on Main Street (Routes 16 & 302), just a short walk from the shops and fine restaurants in the village of North Conway, and close to the seasonal activities in the Mt. Washington Valley. Lea Greenwood and Tom Carter, keepers of the Eastman Inn, will make your stay a memorable one.

Eastman Inn Bed & Breakfast
Box 882, Main Street
Route 16, North Conway, NH 03860
603.356.6707
800.626.5855
www.eastmaninn.com
Innkeepers Lea Greenwood and Tom Carter

Cranberry-Banana Bread

Created by Chef Lea Greenwood of the Eastman Inn
Makes 1 loaf

2 cups flour

1 teaspoon baking soda

1 teaspoon salt

1 1/4 cups sugar

1 egg, beaten

1/3 cup fresh orange juice

1/4 cup vegetable oil

2 tablespoons white-wine vinegar

1 teaspoon freshly grated orange
    zest

2/3 cup mashed, ripe bananas

1 1/4 cups chopped cranberries

1 cup chopped walnuts or pecans

Preheat oven to 350 degrees. Grease a 9 x 5 x 3-inch loaf pan. In a large bowl, sift together the flour, baking soda, salt and sugar. In a separate bowl, whisk together the egg, juice, oil, vinegar and zest. Add the egg mixture to the dry ingredients, and combine just until thoroughly moistened. Fold in the bananas, cranberries and nuts. Spread the batter evenly in the prepared pan, and bake for 60 to 70 minutes (mini-loaf pans, 20 to 25 minutes), until a toothpick inserted near the enter comes out clean. Let cool for 10 minutes, then remove from the pan, and transfer to a wire rack to cool completely.

Note: This bread may be frozen.

Strawberry Bread

Created by Chef Tracy Foor of the Mountain Lake Inn
Makes 4 small or 2 large loaves

4 eggs, beaten

2 cups strawberries, hulled and coarsely chopped

1 1/2 cups vegetable oil

3 cups flour

1 teaspoon baking soda

1 teaspoon salt

1 tablespoon ground cinnamon

2 cups sugar

1 1/4 cups chopped pecans, if desired

Preheat oven to 325 degrees. Grease two, 9 x 5 x 3-inch pans or four, 5 x 3 x 2-inch baking pans. In a large bowl, combine the eggs, strawberries and oil. In a medium bowl, sift together the dry ingredients. Add this to the egg mixture, and stir just until the dry ingredients are thoroughly moistened. Stir in the pecans. Divide the batter among the prepared pans. Bake for about 1 hour, until a toothpick inserted near the center comes out dry.

"My guests just love the idea of no butter in this quick bread."

Pear Bread

Created by Chef Bonnie Webb of The Inn on Golden Pond
Serves 10 to 12

1/2 cup (8 tablespoons) margarine or butter, softened

1 cup sugar

2 eggs

2 cups flour

1/2 teaspoon salt

1/2 teaspoon baking soda

1 teaspoon baking powder

1/8 teaspoon grated nutmeg

1/4 cup plain yogurt

1 cup coarsely chopped, ripe pears (about 1 large pear; leave skin on)

1 teaspoon vanilla extract

Preheat oven to 350 degrees. Grease a 9 x 5 x 3-inch loaf pan. In a medium mixing bowl, cream the margarine and sugar. Beat in the eggs, one at a time. In a separate bowl, stir together the flour, salt, baking soda, baking powder and nutmeg. Add the dry ingredients to the egg mixture, alternating with the yogurt. Stir in the pears and vanilla. Pour into the prepared pan, and bake for 1 hour, until a toothpick inserted near the center comes out clean. Turn the bread onto a rack to cool.

Lemon-Thyme Bread

Created by Chef Christine Crowe of The Crowes' Nest
Makes 1 loaf

2 cups flour

1 1/2 teaspoons baking powder

1/4 teaspoon salt

3/4 cup milk

1 tablespoon chopped fresh lemon balm or fresh lemon juice

1 tablespoon chopped fresh lemon thyme or 1 teaspoon dried thyme

1/2 cup (8 tablespoons) butter, softened

1 cup granulated sugar

2 eggs

1 tablespoon grated lemon zest

For the glaze:

1/2 cup confectioners' sugar

2 tablespoons fresh lemon juice

Preheat oven to 325 degrees. Grease and flour a 9 x 5-inch loaf pan. In a medium bowl, combine the flour, baking powder and salt. In a small saucepan, combine the milk, lemon balm and lemon thyme over medium-high heat. Bring to a boil, and then remove from heat. Let stand, covered, until cool.

In a medium mixing bowl, cream the butter. Add the granulated sugar gradually, beating until light and fluffy. Add the eggs, one at a time, beating well after each addition. Add the flour mixture alternately with the milk mixture, beginning and ending with the flour. Stir in the lemon zest.

Pour into the prepared pan. Bake for 50 minutes, or until a toothpick inserted near the center comes out dry. Meanwhile, make the glaze by combining the confectioners' sugar with the lemon juice. Remove the pan to a wire cooling rack, and let cool in the pan for 10 minutes. Pour 1/2 of the glaze over the top. Let cool completely, and pour the rest of the glaze over the bread.

New England Brown Bread

Makes 5 loaves

1 cup light molasses

1/2 cup (packed) brown sugar

4 cups graham flour

2 cups buttermilk, or 2 cups milk
soured with 4 tablespoons lemon
juice

2 tablespoons butter, melted and
cooled

1 heaping teaspoon baking powder

1 teaspoon salt

1 cup raisins

shortening, for the baking cans

Preheat oven to 350 degrees. In a large bowl, mix all the ingredients well. Grease 5 15-ounce cans (soup cans work nicely) well. Fill each can 2/3 full with batter (any fuller, and the cans will run over during baking). Place the cans on the oven rack, and bake for 30 to 60 minutes, until a cake tester inserted near the center comes out clean.

If You Can't Say Anything Nice . . . .

Regarding biscuits too hard to bite through: "Good skeet."

Sweet Cornbread

Created by Chef Mimi Atwood of The Benjamin Prescott Inn

Serves 12

1/2 cup (8 tablespoons) butter, softened

1 cup sugar

2 eggs

3/4 cup yellow cornmeal

1 3/4 cups flour

2 teaspoons baking powder

1/2 teaspoon salt

1 1/4 cups milk

2/3 cup chopped pineapple (fresh or canned)

Preheat oven to 350 degrees. Grease a 9 x 12-inch baking dish. In a large mixing bowl, cream the butter and sugar until smooth. Add the eggs, and beat well. Beat in the cornmeal. Sift together the flour, baking powder and salt. Add this to the egg mixture, alternating with the milk, mixing thoroughly after each addition. Fold in the pineapple.

Pour the mixture into prepared baking dish. Bake for 25 to 35 minutes, or until a knife inserted in the center comes out clean. If you prefer muffins, bake the batter in greased tins for 15 to 20 minutes.

Knight Family Cornbread
Serves 8 to 10

1 17-ounce can cream-style corn

3/4 cup (12 tablespoons) butter, melted and cooled

1 cup (packed) brown sugar

1 cup yellow cornmeal

1 cup shredded Cheddar cheese

4 teaspoons baking powder

4 eggs, lightly beaten

1 teaspoon salt

1 cup flour

Preheat oven to 350 degrees. Grease a 9 x 13-inch baking pan. In a large mixing bowl, combine all the ingredients. Mix on low speed until well blended. Pour the batter into the prepared baking pan. Bake for 40 to 60 minutes, until the top is slightly golden-brown and a toothpick inserted into the center comes out clean.

No-knead Light Rolls
Makes 18 2-inch rolls

1 1/4-ounce packages dry yeast

1/4 cup 85-degree water

1/4 cup (4 tablespoons) butter, softened

1 1/4 teaspoons salt

2 tablespoons sugar

1 cup boiling water

1 egg, at room temperature

2 1/2 cups sifted flour

In a small bowl, combine the yeast with the 85-degree water; stir to dissolve thoroughly, and let rest in a draft-free place for 10 minutes. Meanwhile, in a medium-large bowl, combine the butter, salt and sugar. Add the boiling water, and stir until the salt and sugar are dissolved. When this mixture has cooled to 85 degrees, add the yeast mixture and egg, and stir with a wooden spoon to combine. Add the flour, and stir to make a soft dough. Transfer the dough to a large, buttered bowl, then with your hand scoop the dough over so the uppermost surface has been buttered. Cover the bowl with a damp cloth. Refrigerate for 2 to 12 hours.

Punch the dough down. With floured hands, pinch off 18 equal pieces of dough. Roll each into a ball, and place them 2 inches apart on 2 greased cookie sheets. Cover with lightly floured towel, and place in a draft-free location. Let the dough rise until about double in bulk.

Preheat oven to 425 degrees. Bake for 14 to 18 minutes, until golden in color.

Italian Bread

Makes 2 loaves

2 1/4-ounce package active dry yeast

1/2 cup warm water

2 cups hot water

3 tablespoons sugar

1 tablespoon salt

1/3 cup vegetable oil

6 cups flour

1 egg white, lightly beaten

sesame seeds (optional)

In a small bowl, dissolve the yeast in the warm water. In a large bowl, combine the hot water, sugar, salt, oil, and 3 cups of the flour. Stir well. Stir in the yeast mixture. Add the remaining flour, and stir to combine. Let the dough rest for 10 minutes; stir it down, and let it rest another 10 minutes. Repeat this process 3 more times (5 times in all). Turn the dough onto a lightly floured board, and knead it only enough to coat the dough with flour so it can be handled. Divide it into 2 equal parts. Roll each part into a 12 x 9-inch rectangle. Then, starting at the long side, roll each rectangle up like a jelly roll. Arrange the loaves on a greased baking sheet, seam-side down, allowing room for both loaves to rise. Let rise in a warm place for 30 minutes, covered with a kitchen towel.

Preheat oven to 400 degrees. With a very sharp knife, cut 3 diagonal gashes across the top of each loaf. Brush with egg white, and sprinkle with sesame seeds, if desired. Bake for about 30 minutes, until the crust is brown. For added crustiness, place a pan of hot water on the floor of the oven during baking.

What is a "flatlander"?

To a Vermonter, a flatlander is someone from New York State. To a Mainer, a flatlander is someone from New Hampshire or Massachusetts or anyplace south of Portland. To a New Hampshirite, a flatlander is someone from Massachusetts, except those from the North Country, to whom flatlanders are anyone from south of Dixville Notch, except to those who inhabit the weather station on top of the Rockpile (a.k.a. Mount Washington). To these brave and hardy souls a flatlander is anybody who ain't them.

Index

A

Acorn Squash Crepes, 49
Angel Egg Puff, 13
Appetizers
    Acorn Squash Crepes, 49
    Fabulous Mushroom Dip, 47
    Gougères (Cheese Puffs), 41
    Hot Crab Wedges, 42
    Hot Swiss Wedges, 42
    Lobster Bomb, 44
    Mountain Lake Inn's Meatballs, 50
    Shrimp Spread, 45
    Skinny Chicken, 52
    Taco Dip, 51
    Tomato-stuffed Mushrooms, 46
    Willow Bend Boursin, 43
Apple Grand Marnier Sauce for French
    Toast, 28
Apple Meat Loaf, 137
Apples
    Apple Crisp, 179
    Apple Fritters, 186
    Apricot-Apple Compote, 183
    Cheese-baked Apples, 35
    Classic Apple Crisp, 178
    Cream of Pumpkin and Apple Soup, 64
    Dutch Apple Cake, 161
    Grandma's Apple Pie, 152
    Harvest Cake, 160
Apricot-Apple Compote, 183
Apricot-brandy Pound Cake, 165
Artichokes
    Gould Hill Pasta, 101
Asparagus
    Crab and Asparagus Soup, 67
Atwood Inn Blueberry Muffins, 217
Atwood Inn Breakfast Pudding, 10
Atwood Inn Breakfast Scones, 216
Atwood Inn Oatmeal Pancakes, 21

B

Baked French Toast, 28
Baked Indian Pudding, 170
Bananas
    Barb's Baked Bananas, 37
    Cranberry-Banana Bread, 225
Basil
    Perfect Pesto, 96
Beans
    Baked Beans, 112
    New Hampshire Baked Beans, 110
Beef
    Apple Meat Loaf, 137
    Beef Tenderloin with Herb-roasted
        Vegetables, 140
    Corned Beef Salad Mold, 85
    Cumin and Molasses Charred Beef
        Tenderloin, 139
    French Oven Beef Stew, 76
    Gram's Tourtière Pie, 136
    Mom's Beef Stew, 74
    Mountain Lake Inn's Meatballs, 50
    Savory Chili, 135
    Whiting Meat Loaf, 138
    Winter Beef Stew, 75
Benjamin's Best Sweet Strada, 11
Bill's French Toast, 25
Blueberries
    Atwood Inn Blueberry Muffins, 217
    Best Blueberry Cobbler, 180
    Blueberry and Lemon Yogurt Soup, 190
    Blueberry Hot Bread, 222
    Blueberry-stuffed French Toast, 26
    Streusel-topped Blueberry Cake, 31
Boston Seaside Salad, 83
Breads *(also see Muffins and Scones)*
    Blueberry Hot Bread, 222
    Caraway Cheese Muffins, 220
    Cranberry-Banana Bread, 225
    Italian Bread, 233

Knight Family Cornbread, 231
Lemon-Thyme Bread, 228
Never-Fail Popovers, 221
New England Brown Bread, 229
No-knead Light Rolls, 232
Pear Bread, 227
Pumpkin Bread, 223
Strawberry Bread, 226
Sweet Cornbread, 230
Breakfast *(also see Muffins and Breads)*
Casserole
Benjamin's Best Sweet Strada, 11
Cereals
Apple-cranberry Granola, 9
Coffee Cake
Jackson Cherry Coffee Cake, 29
Jewish Coffee Cake, 30
Overnight Coffee Cake, 33
Rhubarb Coffee Cake, 32
Streusel-topped Blueberry Cake, 31
Eggs
Angel Egg Puff, 13
Breakfast Casserole, 12
Eggs Benedict Soufflés, 14
Governor's Eggs, 17
Sara's Egg Dish, 16
French Toast
Apple Grand Marnier Sauce for
French Toast, 28
Baked French Toast, 28
Bill's French Toast, 25
Blueberry-stuffed French Toast, 26
Mom's Cinnamon French Toast
with Strawberry-Rhubarb, 27
Fruit
Barb's Baked Bananas, 37
Cheese-baked Apples, 35
Poached Pears with Raspberry
Sauce, 36

Grits
Yankee Grit(s), 34
Muffins
Atwood Inn Blueberry Muffins, 217
Lemon-Lime Muffins, 219
Rhubarb Muffins, 218
Pancakes
Atwood Inn Oatmeal Pancakes, 21
Christine's Baked Apple Pancake, 18
Lemon Souffle Pancakes with
Blueberry Maple Syrup, 24
Pumpkin Pancakes, 19
Walnut Pancakes with Glazed
Bananas, 22
Pudding
Atwood Inn Breakfast Pudding, 10
Scones
Atwood Inn Breakfast Scones, 216
Oatmeal Scones, 215
Breast of Duck with Pears and Grand
Marnier, 127
Bretton Arms, 188
Browned Potatoes, 93
Brownies
Graham Cracker Brownies, 212
Mark's Brownies, 211

C

Cabbage
Spicy Slaw, 84
Cabernet Inn, 154
Cakes
Apricot-brandy Pound Cake, 165
Choco Dot Pumpkin Cake, 157
Chocolate Fudge Cake, 153
Chocolate Strawberry Shortcake, 158
Cranberry Cake, 163
Dutch Apple Cake, 161
English Toffee Heaven, 156

Index

Harvest Cake, 160
Never-fail Sponge Cake, 155
Pineapple Upside-down Cake, 164
Rhubarb Cake, 162
Cantaloupe
Cantaloupe Yogurt Soup, 190
Caraway Cheese Muffins, 220
Carrots
Carrot and Leek Soup, 57
Casseroles
Benjamin's Best Sweet Strada, 11
Breakfast Casserole, 12
Chicken Casserole, 118
Lila's Clam Pie, 131
Lobster Casserole, 130
Cereals
Apple-cranberry Granola, 9
Cheese
Cheese-baked Apples, 35
Chicken-Pecan Quiche, 113
Fabulous Mushroom Dip, 47
Gougères (Cheese Puffs), 41
Hot Swiss Wedges, 42
Macaroni, Ham and Cheese Salad, 104
Skinny Chicken, 52
Taco Dip, 51
Willow Bend Boursin, 43
Cheese-baked Apples, 35
Cherries
Jackson Cherry Coffee Cake, 29
Chesterfield Inn, 48
Chicken
Chicken Casserole, 118
Chicken Dijonnaise, 124
Chicken in Mustard Sauce, 120
Chicken Monadnock, 121
Chicken with Wild Mushrooms and
Artichokes, 119
Chicken-Pecan Quiche, 113
Skinny Chicken, 52
Wolfeboro Inn Pecan Chicken with
Franjelico Sauce, 123
Wolfe's Tavern Varney Island Chicken
Sandwich, 117
Chicken Senegalese Soup, 58
Chili
Savory Chili, 135
Chocolate
Chocolate Chews, 193
Chocolate Fudge Cake, 153
Chocolate Strawberry Shortcake, 158
Graham Cracker Brownies, 212
Kargatton Kisses, 196
Mark's Brownies, 211
Mocha Fudge Cookies, 194
Mocha Stars, 195
Valley Farm's Very Best Chocolate Chip
Cookie, 197
Chowder (also see Soups and Stews)
Corn Chowder, 73
Lobster Chowda' with Smoked
Bacon, 70
Quick Corn Chowder, 72
Smoked Trout, Sweet Potato, and Corn
Chowder, 71
Christine's Baked Apple Pancake, 18
Christine's Hot Fruit Compote, 182
Christmas Thumbprint Cookies, 202
Clams
Lila's Clam Pie, 131
Classic Apple Crisp, 178
Coconut
German Chocolate Cake Frosting, 153
Marvelous Macaroons, 203
Coffee Buttercrunch Pie, 150
Coffee Cake
Jackson Cherry Coffee Cake, 29
Jewish Coffee Cake, 30
Overnight Coffee Cake, 33
Rhubarb Coffee Cake, 32
Streusel-topped Blueberry Cake, 31

Cookies & Sweets
  Chocolate Chews, 193
  Christmas Thumbprint Cookies, 202
  Coriander Cookies, 198
  Fig Squares, 207
  Graham Cracker Brownies, 212
  Grandma Bruno's Brown Sugar
    Rocks, 201
  Grandmother's Oatmeal Cookies, 204
  Kargatton Kisses, 196
  Mark's Brownies, 211
  Marvelous Macaroons, 203
  Mocha Fudge Cookies, 194
  Mocha Stars, 195
  Old-Fashioned Molasses Cookies, 200
  Peanut Butter Cookies, 205
  Peanut Butter Fudge, 209
  Pumpkin Cookies, 199
  Toffee Shortbread, 206
  Valley Farm's Very Best Chocolate Chip
    Cookie, 197
  Welsh Cakes, 208
Corn
  Corn and Chive Pudding, 87
  Corn Casserole, 86
  Corn Chowder, 73
  Knight Family Cornbread, 231
  Quick Corn Chowder, 72
  Smoked Trout, Sweet Potato, and Corn
    Chowder, 71
  Sweet Cornbread, 230
Corned Beef Salad Mold, 85
Crab
  Crab and Asparagus Soup, 67
Cranberries
  Cranberry Cake, 163
  Cranberry-Banana Bread, 225
  Cranberry-Orange Relish, 97
Cranberry Poached Pears, 184
Cream of Pumpkin and Apple Soup, 64
Crème Celeste with Raspberry Sauce, 173

Crisps & Cobblers
  Apple Crisp, 179
  Best Blueberry Cobbler, 180
  Classic Apple Crisp, 178
  Rhubarb Crisp, 177
  Strawberry-Rhubarb Cobbler, 181
Cumin and Molasses Charred Beef
    Tenderloin, 139
Curried Fruit and Nut Salad, 79

D

Dates
  Sherried Date Pudding, 169
Desserts (*also see Pies, Cakes, Puddings, Crisps
    & Cobblers and Cookies & Sweets*)
  Apple Fritters, 186
  Apricot-Apple Compote, 183
  Blueberry and Lemon Yogurt Soup, 190
  Cantaloupe Yogurt Soup, 190
  Christine's Hot Fruit Compote, 182
  Cranberry Poached Pears, 184
  Crème Celeste with Raspberry
    Sauce, 173
  Frozen Raspberry Soufflé, 187
  Honey-Thyme Ice Cream, 189
  Kahlua Tiramisu, 175
  Lily's Puff Pastry, 176
  Poached Pears, 185
  Pumpkin Crème Brulée, 174
  Rhubarb Crisp, 177
Duck
  Breast of Duck with Pears and Grand
    Marnier, 127
  Duck Bombay, 125
  Grilled Breast of Duck with Elderberry
    Chutney and Sweet Potato Hash, 126
  Seared Duck Salad, 82
Dutch Apple Cake, 161

Index

E

Eastman Inn Bed & Breakfast, 224
Eggplant
  Roasted Red Pepper Eggplant Soup, 66
Eggs
  Angel Egg Puff, 13
  Breakfast Casserole, 12
  Chicken-Pecan Quiche, 113
  Eggs Benedict Soufflés, 14
  Governor's Eggs, 17
  Sara's Egg Dish, 16
  Spinach-Rice Frittata, 109
Elderberries
  Grilled Breast of Duck with Elderberry
    Chutney and Sweet Potato Hash, 126
English Toffee Heaven, 156

F

Fabulous Mushroom Dip, 47
Farmstand Tomato Soup, 63
Fiddleheads
  New Hampshire Spring Pasta Toss, 107
Fig Squares, 207
Fish
  Sea Bass with Chipotle Tartar
    Sauce, 128
  Seafood Scampi, 129
  Smoked Salmon Ravioli, 102
Fluffy Peanutbutter Pie, 149
French Mashed Potatoes, 92
French Oven Beef Stew, 76
French Toast
  Apple Grand Marnier Sauce for French
    Toast, 28
  Baked French Toast, 28
  Bill's French Toast, 25
  Blueberry-stuffed French Toast, 26

Mom's Cinnamon French Toast with
  Strawberry-Rhubarb Compote, 27
Frosting
  German Chocolate Cake Frosting, 153
Frozen Raspberry Soufflé, 187
Fruit
  Apples
    Apple Crisp, 179
    Apple Fritters, 186
    Apricot-Apple Compote, 183
    Classic Apple Crisp, 178
    Dutch Apple Cake, 161
    Grandma's Apple Pie, 152
    Harvest Cake, 160
  Bananas
    Barb's Baked Bananas, 37
  Blueberries
    Atwood Inn Blueberry Muffins, 217
    Best Blueberry Cobbler, 180
    Blueberry and Lemon Yogurt
    Soup, 190
    Blueberry Hot Bread, 222
  Cantaloupe Yogurt Soup, 190
  Cheese-baked Apples, 35
  Christine's Hot Fruit Compote, 182
  Cranberry-Orange Relish, 97
  Curried Fruit and Nut Salad, 79
  Elderberries
    Grilled Breast of Duck with
      Elderberry Chutney and, 126
  Mango
    Sunshine Mango Salsa, 95
  Pears
    Cranberry Poached Pears, 184
    Pear Bread, 227
    Poached Pears, 185
  Pineapple
    Pineapple Pie, 151
    Pineapple Upside-down Cake, 164

Raspberries
    Crème Celeste with Raspberry
        Sauce, 173
    Frozen Raspberry Soufflé, 187
Strawberries
    Chocolate Strawberry Shortcake, 158
    Strawberry Bread, 226
    Strawberry-Rhubarb Cobbler, 181

G

Gap Mountain Stew, 65
German Chocolate Cake Frosting, 153
Glazed Pork Tenderloin withBraised Red
    Cabbage, 145
Gougères (Cheese Puffs), 41
Gould Hill Pasta, 101
Governor's Eggs, 17
Graham Cracker Brownies, 212
Gram's Grapenut Custard Pudding, 171
Gram's Tourtière Pie, 136
Grandma Bruno's Brown Sugar
    Rocks, 201
Grandma's Apple Pie, 152
Grandmother's Oatmeal Cookies, 204
Grilled Breast of Duck with Elderberry
    Chutney and Sweet Potato Hash, 126
Grilled Seafood Soup, 69

H

Ham
    Macaroni, Ham and Cheese Salad, 104
Harvest Cake, 160
Honey-Thyme Ice Cream, 189
Hot Crab Wedges, 42
Hot Swiss Wedges, 42

I

Inn at East Hill Farm, 210
Inn on Newfound Lake, 106
Italian Bread, 233

J

Jackson Cherry Coffee Cake, 29
Jay's Vinaigrette, 94
Jewish Coffee Cake, 30

K

Kahlua Tiramisu, 175
Karen's Pasta, 105
Kargatton Kisses, 196
Knight Family Cornbread, 231

L

Lamb
    1812 Steakhouse Rack of Lamb with
        Sweet, Garlic Demi-Glace, 146
Leeks
    Carrot and Leek Soup, 57
    Potato Leek Soup, 61
Lemon Souffle Pancakes with Blueberry
    Maple Syrup, 24
Lemon-Lime Muffins, 219
Lemon-Thyme Bread, 228
Lila's Clam Pie, 131
Lily's Puff Pastry, 176
Lobster
    Lobster Bomb, 44
    Lobster Casserole, 130

Index

Lobster Chowda' with Smoked
Bacon, 70
Loin of Pork with Port Sauce, 142
Lynda's Wonton Soup, 56

M

Macaroni, Ham and Cheese Salad, 104
Mandarin Orange Salad with Poppy Seed
Dressing, 81
Mango
Sunshine Mango Salsa, 95
Maple Salad Dressing, 94
Maria Atwood Inn, 20
Mark's Brownies, 211
Marvelous Macaroons, 203
Meat Loaf
Apple Meat Loaf, 137
Whiting Meat Loaf, 138
Meatballs
Mountain Lake Inn's Meatballs, 50
Mocha Fudge Cookies, 194
Mocha Stars, 195
Mom's Beef Stew, 74
Mom's Cinnamon French Toast with
Strawberry-Rhubarb Compote, 27
Mount Washington Hotel
& Resort, 144
Mountain Lake Inn's Meatballs, 50
Muffins *(also see Breads)*
Atwood Inn Blueberry Muffins, 217
Caraway Cheese Muffins, 220
Lemon-Lime Muffins, 219
Rhubarb Muffins, 218
Topping
Useful Streusel, 217
Mushrooms
Fabulous Mushroom Dip, 47
Tomato-stuffed Mushrooms, 46

N

Never-Fail Popovers, 221
Never-fail Sponge Cake, 155
New England Brown Bread, 229
New Hampshire Baked Beans, 110
New Hampshire Spring Pasta Toss, 107
No-knead Light Rolls, 232

O

Oatmeal Scones, 215
Old-Fashioned Molasses Cookies, 200
Onions
Portuguese Onion Soup, 60
Orange-Glazed Pork Loin, 143
Oranges
Cranberry-Orange Relish, 97
Overnight Coffee Cake, 33

P

Pancakes
Atwood Inn Oatmeal Pancakes, 21
Christine's Baked Apple Pancake, 18
Lemon Souffle Pancakes with Blueberry
Maple Syrup, 24
Pumpkin Pancakes, 19
Walnut Pancakes with Glazed
Bananas, 22
Pasta
Gould Hill Pasta, 101
Karen's Pasta, 105
Macaroni, Ham and Cheese Salad, 104
New Hampshire Spring Pasta Toss, 107
Smoked Salmon Ravioli, 102
Zucchini Spaghetti Casserole, 108

Peanut Butter
  Fluffy Peanut Butter Pie, 149
  Peanut Butter Cookies, 205
  Peanut Butter Fudge, 209
Pears
  Cranberry Poached Pears, 184
  Pear Bread, 227
  Poached Pears, 185
  Poached Pears with Raspberry Sauce, 36
Pesto
  Perfect Pesto, 96
Pies
  Coffee Buttercrunch Pie, 150
  Fluffy Peanutbutter Pie, 149
  Grandma's Apple Pie, 152
  Meat
    Gram's Tourtière Pie, 136
  Pineapple Pie, 151
Pineapple Upside-down Cake, 164
Pork
  Glazed Pork Tenderloin with Braised
    Red Cabbage, 145
  Loin of Pork with Port Sauce, 142
  Lynda's Wonton Soup, 56
  Orange-Glazed Pork Loin, 143
  Pork Chops Supreme, 141
Portuguese Onion Soup, 60
Potatoes
  Browned Potatoes, 93
  French Mashed Potatoes, 92
  Potato Leek Soup, 61
  Skinny Chicken, 52
Puddings
  Atwood Inn Breakfast Pudding, 10
  Baked Indian Pudding, 170
  Corn
    Corn and Chive Pudding, 87
  Gram's Grapenut Custard Pudding, 171
  Sherried Date Pudding, 169
  Steamed Pudding with Hard Sauce, 172

Pumpkin
  Choco Dot Pumpkin Cake, 157
  Cream of Pumpkin and Apple Soup, 64
  Pumpkin Bread, 223
  Pumpkin Cookies, 199
  Pumpkin Crème Brulée, 174
  Pumpkin Pancakes, 19

Q

Quick and Easy Vegetable Soup, 59
Quick and Perfect Blender Hollandaise, 98
Quick Corn Chowder, 72

R

Raspberries
  Crème Celeste with Raspberry
    Sauce, 173
  Frozen Raspberry Soufflé, 187
Red Peppers
  Roasted Red Pepper Eggplant Soup, 66
Relish
  Cranberry-Orange Relish, 97
Rhubarb
  Rhubarb Cake, 162
  Rhubarb Coffee Cake, 32
  Rhubarb Crisp, 177
  Rhubarb Muffins, 218
Rice
  Spinach-Rice Frittata, 109
Riverview Farms Inn, 90
Rolls
  No-knead Light Rolls, 232

Index

S

Salad Dressings
  Jay's Vinaigrette, 94
  Maple Salad Dressing, 94
Salads
  Boston Seaside Salad, 83
  Corned Beef Salad Mold, 85
  Curried Fruit and Nut Salad, 79
  Macaroni, Ham and Cheese Salad, 104
  Mandarin Orange Salad with Poppy
    Seed Dressing, 81
  Seared Duck Salad, 82
  Spicy Slaw, 84
  Spinach Salad, 80
Salsa
  Sunshine Mango Salsa, 95
Sandwiches
  Wolfe's Tavern Varney Island Chicken
    Sandwich, 117
Sara's Egg Dish, 16
Sauce
  Apple Grand Marnier Sauce for French
    Toast, 28
  Quick and Perfect Blender
    Hollandaise, 98
Sausage
  Karen's Pasta, 105
Savory Chili, 135
Scalloped Tomatoes, 88
Scones
  Atwood Inn Breakfast Scones, 216
  Oatmeal Scones, 215
Seafood
  Boston Seaside Salad, 83
  Crab and Asparagus Soup, 67
  Grilled Seafood Soup, 69
  Hot Crab Wedges, 42
  Lila's Clam Pie, 131
  Lobster Bomb, 44
  Lobster Casserole, 130
  Lobster Chowda' with Smoked
    Bacon, 70
  New Hampshire Spring Pasta Toss, 107
  Sea Bass with Chipotle Tartar
    Sauce, 128
  Seafood Scampi, 129
  Shrimp Spread, 45
  Smoked Salmon Ravioli, 102
  Smoked Trout, Sweet Potato, and Corn
    Chowder, 71
Seared Duck Salad, 82
Sherried Date Pudding, 169
Skinny Chicken, 52
Soup *(also see Chowders and Stews)*
  Blueberry and Lemon Yogurt Soup, 190
  Cantaloupe Yogurt Soup, 190
  Carrot and Leek Soup, 57
  Chicken Senegalese Soup, 58
  Crab and Asparagus Soup, 67
  Cream of Pumpkin and Apple Soup, 64
  Farmstand Tomato Soup, 63
  Gap Mountain Stew, 65
  Grilled Seafood Soup, 69
  Lynda's Wonton Soup, 56
  Portuguese Onion Soup, 60
  Potato Leek Soup, 61
  Quick and Easy Vegetable Soup, 59
  Roasted Red Pepper Eggplant Soup, 66
  Smoked Trout, Sweet Potato, and Corn
    Chowder, 71
  Sweet Chestnut Soup, 55
  Woodbine Tomato Soup, 62
Spinach
  Spinach Salad, 80
  Spinach-Rice Frittata, 109
Squash
  Acorn Squash Crepes, 49
Steakhouse Rack of Lamb with Sweet,
    Garlic Demi-Glace, 146
Steamed Pudding with Hard Sauce, 172

Stew *(also see Chowders and Soups)*
    French Oven Beef Stew, 76
    Gap Mountain Stew, 65
    Mom's Beef Stew, 74
    Winter Beef Stew, 75
Strawberries
    Chocolate Strawberry Shortcake, 158
    Strawberry Bread, 226
    Strawberry-Rhubarb Cobbler, 181
Streusel-topped Blueberry Cake, 31
Sunset Hill House, 68
Sunshine Mango Salsa, 95
Sweet Cornbread, 230
Sweet Potatoes
    Smoked Trout, Sweet Potato, and Corn
        Chowder, 71
    Sweet Potato Hash, 89
    Sweet Potato Pie, 91

T

Taco Dip, 51
Toffee Shortbread, 206
Tomato-stuffed Mushrooms, 46
Tomatoes
    Farmstand Tomato Soup, 63
    Scalloped Tomatoes, 88
    Woodbine Tomato Soup, 62
Toppings
    Useful Streusel, 217

U

Useful Streusel, 217

V

Valley Farm's Very Best Chocolate Chip
    Cookie, 197
Vegetables
  Artichokes
    Gould Hill Pasta, 101
  Cabbage
    Spicy Slaw, 84
  Corn
    Corn and Chive Pudding, 87
  Potatoes
    Browned Potatoes, 93
    French Mashed Potatoes, 92
  Pumpkin
    Pumpkin Crème Brulée, 174
  Quick and Easy Vegetable Soup, 59
  Spinach
    Spinach-Rice Frittata, 109
  Sweet Potatoes
    Sweet Potato Pie, 91
    Sweet Potato Hash, 89
  Tomatoes
    Scalloped Tomatoes, 88
  Zucchini
    Zucchini Spaghetti Casserole, 108

W

Walnut Pancakes with Glazed Bananas and
    Spiced Crème Fraîche, 22
Welsh Cakes, 208
Whiting Meat Loaf, 138
Willow Bend Boursin, 43
Winter Beef Stew, 75
Wolfeboro Inn, 122

Index

Wolfeboro Inn Pecan Chicken with
  Franjelico Sauce, 123
Wolfe's Tavern Varney Island Chicken
  Sandwich, 117
Woodbine Tomato Soup, 62

Y

Yankee Grit(s), 34

Z

Zucchini
  Zucchini Spaghetti Casserole, 108

The Hearth

One of the beautiful homes built shortly after the construction of the old Hopkinton Court House was the center chimney Georgian-style house of bucklemaker Moses Emery. Its enormous brick hearth, (found on the title page) measuring nine feet wide and four feet high, is said to be one of the biggest in New Hampshire. The two beehive ovens flanking the fireplace must have been the cutting edge of kitchen design at the time.

To bake in one of these ovens the lady of the house would have been required to use her own arm to judge its temperature. She would stick her arm inside and count the number of seconds (or perhaps the number of Doxology verses) for which she could keep it there. Experience, and probably her own mother's example, taught her when the oven was ready for the task at hand.

It wasn't only private fare that women prepared in this cavernous fireplace, however. In the early 19th century, when the Court House next door was still teeming with political activity, those who lived in this home had a tavern license. Presumably legislators, jurors (or even judges) found it a handy spot to partake of liquid refreshment such as a steaming noggin of flip - beer, molasses and rum heated by a red-hot poker.

Cooking over an open fire for either the public or for family was physically demanding and extremely dangerous. Women had to be constantly vigilant that their long, full skirts, not to mention their mischievous toddlers, were kept safely away from the flames and coals. It wasn't until the iron cookstove came into use in the 1830s that women could finally cook standing up, with their clothing and children shielded from the flames.

RUTH CHEVION

Ruth Chevion follows a Feng Shui philosophy in her work: subjects and colors are intended to contribute to a sense of harmony. She specializes in still life and local country scenes using the traditional oil-paint method of the Flemish masters. She works at the New Light Studio in the historic town of Hopkinton.

Contributing Artists

Byron Carr - bcarr@conknet.com

Sally Chase - 603.746.4798

Ruth Chevion - rchevion@nh.ultranet.com

Tamara Craig - avectbc@mediaone.net

Ellen Davis - 603.746.5664

Mary French - johnfrench@mediaone.net

Audrey Gardner - agardner@nh.ultranet.com

Andre Hurtgen - ahurtgen@yahoo.com

Jane List - jlist@nh.ultranet.com

Marjorie Noon - 603.746.4827

Sandy Strang - 603.746.6537

Charlotte Thibault - 603.746.3125

Student Art:

Taryn Craig - Rendering of Butterfly Motif

Giselle Harrington - Rendering of Sheep

Will Merrow - Rendering of Owl

Dianne Pfundstein - Rendering of Lilacs

A special thank you to the participating inns for their recipes and support.

The pen and ink drawings of the featured inns found throughout our book were rendered by Sandy Strang, a professional artist who lives in Contoocook, New Hampshire.

Participating Inns

The Benjamin Prescott Inn
433 Turnpike Road
East Jaffrey, NH 03452
(603) 532-6637
Fax: (603) 532-6637
E-mail: bprescottinn@aol.com
Owner: Mimi Atwood

The Bretton Arms Country Inn
at The Mount Washington Resort
Route 302
Bretton Woods, NH 03575
(800) 258-0330
(603) 278-1000
Fax: (603) 278-8838
www.mtwashington.com

Cabernet Inn
Route 16 at the Intervale
P.O. Box 489
North Conway, NH 03860
(603) 356-4704
Fax: (603) 356-5399
E-mail: info@cabernetinn.com
www.cabernetinn.com
Owners: Debbie and Rich Howard

Carter Notch Inn
Carter Notch RD
Jackson, NH 03846
(603) 383-9630
Fax: (603) 383-9642
E-mail: dunwell@landmarnet.net
Owners: Lynda and Jim Dunwell

Chester Field Inn
P.O. Box 155
Chesterfield, NH 03443
(800) 365-5515
(603) 256-3211
Fax: (603) 256-6131
E-mail: chstinn@sover.net
www.chesterfieldinn.com
Owners: Judy and Phil Hueber

The Crowes' Nest
Thorn Mountain Road
P.O. Box 427
Jackson, NH 03846
(603) 383-8913
Fax: (603) 383-8241
E-mail: crowesnest@landmarknet.net
Owners:Myles and Christine Crowe

The Darby Field Country Inn and Restaurant
185 Chase Hill RD
Conway, NH 03818
(603) 447-2181
Fax: (603) 447-5726
E-mail: marc@darbyfield.com
Owners: Marc and Maria Donaldson

Eastman Inn
P.O. Box 882
Main Street, Route 16
N. Conway, NH 03860
(603) 356-6707
Fax: (603) 356-7708
E-mail: info@eastmaninn.com
www.eastmaninn.com
Owners: Lea Greenwood and
    Tom Carter

Enchanted Nights Bed and Breakfast
Coastal Rte. 103
Kittery, ME 03904
(207) 439-1489
E-mail: info@enchanted-nights-bandb.com
Owners: Nancy Bogerberger and Peter Lamandia

Ferry Point House B&B
Lake Winnisquam
100 Lower Bay RD
Sanbornton, NH 03269
(603) 524-0087
Fax: (603) 524-0959
E-mail: ferrypt@together.net
Owners: Joe and Diane Damato

The Inn at East Hill Farm
460 Monadnock
Troy, NH 03465
(603) 242-6495
Fax: (603) 242-7709
E-mail: info@easthillfarm.com
Owners: Sally and Dave Adams

The Inn at Portsmouth Harbor
6 Walter ST
Kittery, ME 03904
(603) 439-4040
Fax: (207) 438-9286
E-mail: info@innatportsmouth.com
Owners: Kim and Terry O'Mahoney

Inn at Valley Farms
B&B Cottages
633 Wentworth RD
Walpole, NH 03608
(603) 756-2855
Fax: (603) 756-2865
E-Mail: info@innatvalleyfarms.com
Owner: Jacqueline Badders

The Inn on Golden Pond
P.O. Box 680
Route 3
Holderness, NH 03245
(603) 968-7269
Fax: (603) 968-9226
E-mail: innongp@lr.net
Owners: Bonnie and Bill Webb

The Inn on Newfound Lake
Route 3A
Bridgewater, NH 03222
(603) 744-9111
Fax: (603) 744-3894
E-mail: inonlk@cyberportal.net
Owner: Phelps C. Boyce

The Manor on Golden Pond
Rte 3, Box T
Holderness, NH 03245
(603) 968-3348
Fax: (603) 968-2116
E-mail: manorinn@lr.net
Owners: Jeffrey Woolley

Maple Hedge
355 Main ST
P.O. Box 638
Charlestown, New Hampshire 03603
(603) 826-5237
Fax: (603) 826-5237
E-mail: debrine@fmis.net
Owner: Joan DeBrine

Maple Hill Farm
200 Newport RD
New London, NH 03257
(603) 526-2248
(800) 231-8637
Fax: (603) 526-4170
E-Mail: daufranc@kear.net
Owners: Dennis and Roberta Aufranc

The Maria Atwood Inn
71 Hill RD
Route 3A
Franklin, NH 03235
(603) 934-3666
E-mail: atwoodinn@cyberportal.net
www.atwoodinn.com
Owners: Sandi and Fred Hoffmeister

Mountain Lake Inn
2871 Rte. 114
Bradford, NH 03221
(603) 938-2136
(800) 662-6005
Fax: (603) 938-5622
E-Mail: rfoor@conknet.com
Owners: Bob and Tracy Foor

Mt. Chocorua View House
Rt. 16, Box 395
Chocorua, NH 03817
(603) 323-8350
Fax: (603) 323-3319
Email: fbholmes@landmarknet.net
Owners: Frank and Barbara Holmes

Mount Washington Hotel and Resort
Route 302
Bretton Woods, NH 03575
(603) 278-1000
Fax: (603) 278-8828
E-mail: rcarson@mtwashington.com
www.mtwashington.com
Owner: Mount Washington Preservation

The Red Sleigh Inn Bed & Breakfast
P.O. Box 562
Pollard Road
Lincoln, New Hampshire 03251
(603) 745-8517
E-mail: redsleigh@linwoodnet.com
Owners: Michael and Patricia McGuinn

Riverview Farms Inn
1 Village RD
Wilmot Flat, NH 03287
(603) 526-4482
Fax: (603) 526-2995
E-mail: mpacetta@tds.net
www.newlondon-nh.com
Owner: M. A. Pacetta

The 1785 Inn and Restaurant
Rte. 16
North Conway, NH 03860
(603) 356-9025
(800) 421-1785
Fax: (603) 356-6081
E-mail: the1785inn@aol.com
Owner: Charlie and Becky Mallar

Stepping Stones B&B
6 Bennington Battle Trail
Wilton Center, NH 03086
(603) 654-9048
E-Mail: anncarlsmith@mymailstation
www.steppingstones.com
Owner: D. Ann Carlsmith

Stonewall Farm B & B
235 Windsor RD
Hillsborough, NH 03244
(603) 478-1947
Fax: (603) 478-5227
E-mail: stonewall_farm@hotmail.com
Owner: Meg Curtis

Sunset Hill House
231 Sunset Hill RD
Sugar Hill, NH 03585
(800) 786-4455
(603) 823-5522
Fax: (603) 823-5738
E-mail: innkeepers@sunsethillhouse.com
www.sunsethillhouse.com
Owners: Nancy and Lon Henderson

Whitneys' Inn
Route 16B, P.O. Box 822
Jackson, NH 03846
(603) 383-8916
Fax: (603) 383-6886
www.whitneysinn.com
Owner: Robert Bowman

Wolfeboro Inn
90 North Main Street
Wolfeboro, NH 03894
(603) 569-3016
Fax: (603) 569-5375
www.wolfeboroinn.com

The Hopkinton Woman's Club would like to thank the following sponsors that helped to fund the printing of this cookbook.

Jane Bradstreet
Hopkinton, New Hampshire

Concord Litho
Concord, New Hampshire

Theresa and Kenneth DeWitt
Hopkinton, New Hampshire

Excalibur Shelving Systems, Inc.
Contoocook, New Hampshire

Freudenberg NOK
Manchester, New Hampshire

Herrick Millwork, Inc.
Contoocook, New Hampshire

Cynthia Martin
Meredith, New Hampshire

MCT Telcom
Contoocook, New Hampshire

New Hampshire Charitable Foundation
Concord, New Hampshire

New Kearsarge Corporation
Contoocook, New Hampshire

Historical Notes

Dorothea Jensen, who wrote the text accompanying the artwork in this book, is the author of The Riddle of Penncroft Farm, a children's novel about the American Revolution, published by Harcourt. She has lived in Contoocook since 1991. She would like to thank Rose Hanson for generously sharing her files and her memories, Elaine Loft for helping sift through New Hampshire Antiquarian Society publications and files, Ashton Bohanon for his exciting account of the flood of 1936, and Steve Thomas for providing excerpts from his upcoming church history and other information.

Additional sources used for these pieces include:

Carlo, Joyce W. *Trammels, Trenchers, & Tartlets*. Old Saybrook: Peregrine Press, 1982.

Fennelly, Catherine. *Country Stores in Early New England*. Sturbridge: OSV, 1955.

Heald, Bruce. "The Timbers of the Kearsarge", "The Alabama Sunk by the Kearsarge", *The Weirs Times*, April, 2001.

Lord, C.C. *Life and Times in Hopkinton*. NHAS, 1890. (1970 update by Rose Hanson.)

MacIntire, Jane Bacon. *Lafayette, the Guest of the Nation*. Newton: Simone Press, 1967.

Pratt, Ned. *Main Street, Hopkinton, NH: an Architectural Walking Tour*. NHAS, 2000.

A Walk Through Two Villages: Contoocook and Hopkinton. NHAS, 1990.

Yesterday and Today, An Illustrated Historical Account of the Town of Hopkinton, New Hampshire 1765-1965. NHAS, 1965.

Cookbook Committee

Karen Barnhart - Chairman
Jane Bradstreet - Marketing
Rebecca Briccetti - Editor
Sally Church - Advisor
Tammy Clay - Recipe Testing
Tamara Craig - Art and Artists
Betsy Douglas - Editing and Proof-reading
Alex Lawrence - Treasurer and Inventory
Pam McDonald - Sponsorship
Stella Rideout - Advisor
Cathy Rothwell - Advisor
Pat Smith - Data Entry
Melisa Weber - Editing and Copyright

This cookbook represents the talents and time of many dedicated individuals from the Hopkinton Community. Without their support and hard work in large and small ways over the past two years, its publication would not have been possible. We want to thank all who shared their recipes and regret that space constraints and duplications precluded us from including all of the wonderful recipes that we received. Please know that your contributions were appreciated. Thank you to all who spent hours testing and evaluating recipes, editing, typing, and proofing the text. Thank you to all of the artists and writers who came together in spirit to form what we think is a wonderful collection of New Hampshire art and stories. Thank you to the innkeepers and professional chefs who had the faith that the quality of our cookbook would do justice to their inn and their recipes. Thank you to the individuals, businesses and organizations that financially supported the initial printing of the book. Thank you to all who will continue to help in the future to support this book and continue its success. We apologize if we have inadvertently omitted any names from our list of contributors.

Additional Contributions

The New Hampshire
  Antiquarian Society
Diane Avery
Pat Ayers
Melissa Barry
Kathleen Belko
Larry Bickford
Michelle Bickford
Elizabeth Bloomquist
Mary Boss
Khristin Carroll
Lois Carroll
Jane Cate
Michelle Cavallaro
Kathy Chamberlin
EH Chase
Valerie Chittim
Nancy Clark
Georgie Comstock
Jan Davio
Sue Davis
Theresa DeWitt
Betty Dibble
Shannon Donahue
Karen Dufault
Shirley Dunlop
Linda Dunning
Martha Erickson

Susan Gagnon
Donna Gould
Joan Gourley
Lisa Hall
Chris Hamm
Martha Healy
Celeste Hemingson
Peg Herbert
Patty Howland
Martha Johnson
Melissa Jones
Marie Keane
Audrey Knight
Barbara Langworth
Linda Lee
Kelly Lewis
Valerie Lynn
Cindy Martin
Sara McNeil
Lisa Metzger
Mary Jane Miller
Mary Mitchell
Diane Myler
Sally Patenaude
Susan Perrin
Gail Piatt
Leeann Pierce
Geneva Pinckney

E. Quinn
Marilyn Rogers
Ida Mae Rondeau
Elizabeth Rothwill
Rebecca Rule
George Sabol
Suzanne Sauer
Elizabeth Seales
Helen Todd Selvin
Ruth Shedd
Janice Sheen
Irene Shepard
Holli Siff
Ann Simms
Anne Slusser
Spring Ledge
Farmstand
Shannan Tawney
Kathy Thesing
Lauren Vallari
Melanie Wheat
Cindy White
Ruthie White
April Whittaker
Dace Winzeler
Nan Winzeler
Susan Yonkers
Joan York
Natalie Zook

New Hampshire Fun

Popular speaker and humorist Rebecca Rule wrote the "New Hampshire witticisms" that are scattered throughout this book and are denoted by the butterflies. A recipient of the "Emerging Writer" award from the New Hampshire Writers Project, Rebecca is the author of *Wood Heat*, and co-author with Susan Wheeler of *Creating the Story: Guide for Writers* and *True Stories: Guide for Writing from your Life* (Heinemann). Rebecca's original plays include *Town Meeting: The Musical* and *The History of Wakefield: A Comedy*. Available on audiotape are: *Perley Gets a Dump Sticker and other Harrowing Tales, Fishing With George: True stories and Tolerable Lies,* and *The Widow and the Trapper: Stories of New England* (Audio Bookshelf).

For more information on any of these programs or her personal appearances, please contact Rebecca Rule at: butterflea@aol.com

Or write: Rebecca Rule
178 Mountain Avenue
Northwood, NH 03261

Stone Walls and Warm Hearths

THE INNS AND OUTS OF EATING IN NEW HAMPSHIRE

P.O. Box 24
Hopkinton, New Hampshire 03229
Toll-free Telephone or Fax: 1-866-HWC-COOK
E-mail: stonewalls@mediaone.net
Visit us on the web at www.stonewalls.org

Name _____

Address _____

City _____ State _____ Zip _____

Please send me _____ copies   @ 22.95each _____

Postage and handling   @   4.00each _____

Gift wrap and note card _____ copies   @   3.00each _____

Total Enclosed   _____

Please make checks payable to Hopkinton Woman's Club

Please charge my account (circle one):   Visa   Mastercard

Card number: _____ Expiration Date _____

Signature as it appears on the card: _____

To open a retail or wholesale account, please call 1-866-492-2665

- -

Stone Walls and Warm Hearths

THE INNS AND OUTS OF EATING IN NEW HAMPSHIRE

P.O. Box 24
Hopkinton, New Hampshire 03229
Toll-free Telephone or Fax: 1-866-HWC-COOK
E-mail: stonewalls@mediaone.net
Visit us on the web at www.stonewalls.org

Name _____

Address _____

City _____ State _____ Zip _____

Please send me _____ copies   @ 22.95each _____

Postage and handling   @   4.00each _____

Gift wrap and note card _____ copies   @   3.00each _____

Total Enclosed   _____

Please make checks payable to Hopkinton Woman's Club

Please charge my account (circle one):   Visa   Mastercard

Card number: _____ Expiration Date _____

Signature as it appears on the card: _____

To open a retail or wholesale account, please call 1-866-492-2665

Stone Walls and Warm Hearths

THE INNS AND OUTS OF EATING IN NEW HAMPSHIRE

P.O. Box 24
Hopkinton, New Hampshire 03229
Toll-free Telephone or Fax: 1-866-HWC-COOK
E-mail: stonewalls@mediaone.net
Visit us on the web at www.stonewalls.org

Name _____

Address_____

City _____ State _____ Zip _____

Please send me _____ copies   @ 22.95each _____

Postage and handling   @   4.00each_____

Gift wrap and note card _____ copies   @   3.00each_____

Total Enclosed

Please make checks payable to Hopkinton Woman's Club

Please charge my account (circle one):   Visa   Mastercard

Card number: _____ Expiration Date:_____

Signature as it appears on the card: _____

To open a retail or wholesale account, please call 1-866-492-2665

- -

Stone Walls and Warm Hearths

THE INNS AND OUTS OF EATING IN NEW HAMPSHIRE

P.O. Box 24
Hopkinton, New Hampshire 03229
Toll-free Telephone or Fax: 1-866-HWC-COOK
E-mail: stonewalls@mediaone.net
Visit us on the web at www.stonewalls.org

Name _____

Address_____

City_____State _____ Zip _____

Please send me _____ copies   @ 22.95each _____

Postage and handling   @   4.00each _____

Gift wrap and note card _____ copies   @   3.00each _____

Total Enclosed   _____

Please make checks payable to Hopkinton Woman's Club

Please charge my account (circle one):   Visa   Mastercard

Card number: _____ Expiration Date:_____

Signature as it appears on the card:_____

To open a retail or wholesale account, please call 1-866-492-2665